Advance Praise for
Problem Child

"Terrell, we're still feeling the goosebumps."

—QUINCY JONES

"My beautiful baby boy, even more beautiful on the inside, and he sings even better than that. Now Ms. Patti is giving him his wings to fly among the greats."

—PATTI LaBELLE

problem child

problem child

TERRELL CARTER
WITH STACY THUNES

Post Hill
PRESS

A POST HILL PRESS BOOK

Problem Child
© 2020 by Terrell Carter
All Rights Reserved

ISBN: 978-1-64293-431-1
ISBN (eBook): 978-1-64293-432-8

Cover photo by Clyph Jean-Philippe
Interior design and composition, Greg Johnson, Textbook Perfect

Post Hill Press
New York • Nashville
posthillpress.com
Published in the United States of America

*This book is dedicated to the memories of
Lela Carter, Oda-Lee Clay, and Mae Burder.*

contents

Part Two

prologue

In the beginning God created the heavens and the Earth. Now the Earth was formless and empty, darkness was over the surface of the deep, and the Spirit of God was hovering over the waters. And God said, "Let there be light," and there was light. God saw that the light was good and he separated the light from the darkness. God called the light "day," and the darkness he called "night." And there was evening, and there was morning—the first day.

—GENESIS, 1–3

Some scientists would have you believe that a bunch of asteroids traveling randomly through space collided into each other with such force that they started a massive rotation we now know as our solar system, and that those nine enormous pieces of rock that randomly collided are now uniformly spinning around a ball of fire. All nine planets started to take on their own identity, as well as becoming perfectly round in shape. Some are frozen over or full of molten rock. One in particular, according to this theory, formed just the right conditions—such as gravity, water, and air—upon which a thing called "life" could emerge and subsequently survive. Some kind of primitive, microscopic organism grew out of this randomness and began to take shape, multiplying and feeding off their surroundings. Over millions of years, these organisms began to collect and form different types of characteristics, from insect to beast to animal, until finally evolving into the human race as we know it today. During this evolutionary period, the Earth continued to revolve around the sun, and even more incredibly, it's still on the same course. Nothing has changed, no random shifting on its axis, no random collisions with other materials. Throughout this evolutionary period, humans developed into such amazing beings that they have not only devised ways to move themselves from one place to the other in moving and flying vehicles, they have created technology that has permitted flight to other planets, like the Moon and Mars. We humans have also created ships and crafts to take us across and to the depths of the sea, and constructed buildings to withstand the elements.

If you'll recall, according to this theory, everything we know, and everything we don't know, came about because of a random coincidence that had to do with some floating rocks that appeared out of nowhere and played bumper cars with each other. Sounds unbelievable, right? Well, maybe that's because it just might be. Personally, I don't believe in coincidences. In other words, I believe that the Big Bang is about as much of a coincidence as the story I'm about to share with you now.

part one

chapter 1

Empire

I was in New York City at the Ritz-Carlton Hotel for one of the most exciting nights of my career so far, waiting for my publicist to let me know that the car had arrived to take me to the premiere for season four of the hit television show *Empire*. I began playing the character Warren Hall in the final episode of season three, cast to play the nephew of Phylicia Rashad and cousin of Taye Diggs. Wow! I couldn't have asked for a better introduction...until my first scene. The camera slowly pans up with a shot of me singing one of the most captivating songs ever, "Born to Love You," to Jussie Smollett who plays Jamal, my love interest on the show. After two months of waiting, I finally got the offer letter and was bumped up to series regular. I realized that this was the opportunity of a lifetime, one I had been working toward my whole life.

So here I was, looking out over the New York skyline, thinking about how far I'd come and how much further I still wanted to go, enjoying the feeling of success that I had worked hard to achieve. It was a huge moment for me, although I have to admit, my mind briefly wandered to the thoughts of the other actors on the show and how, for them, a night like this was almost routine. But not for me. Not yet, anyway. Before this I'd worked with Tyler Perry in his touring theater plays including *Madea's Class Reunion, Meet the Browns,* and *What's Done in the Dark,* and it's where I learned how to really kill it with an audience every night, all of which I owe to Mr. Perry. Tyler's first movie, *Diary of a Mad Black Woman,* was my first film. I played the young pastor singing the soul-stirring gospel song "Father Can You Hear Me." This movie went straight to number one, which I still regard as being nothing less than miraculous.

But tonight was all about *Empire,* man. What a show, a forerunner in black entertainment, going mainstream for all audiences, of all colors and backgrounds. I loved watching it and now I was a *part* of it. In my heart and soul, I knew this was a portent of greater things to come as I stood there feeling like, fuck yeah, I've worked my ass off to get where I am, and now I'm ready. I was sure that nothing, not one single thing, could stop me from enjoying this night to the fullest. That is, until I noticed a series of Facebook messages light up my phone.

Looking at the display and the names that kept popping up, I noticed various family members and people I haven't heard from in years. Even before I read the messages, something sunk in my soul, hitting me like a Mack truck, and I knew. Momma died. Even though my heart froze, I gotta be honest and tell you my first thought was, *Thank you, Momma, for ruining my night.*

My publicist, who always kept a key to my room, knocked briefly, then came in all excited, gushing, "It's time!" I was silent. "What's wrong?" she asked.

"Momma died," I said without emotion.

"Oh my God, Terrell! Your mother died? I'm so sorry."

"No. Momma was my grandmother."

"You called your grandmother 'Momma'?" she asked, looking at me with empathetic eyes.

"Yeah, she raised me...and Candy. Anyway..." The puzzled look on her face told me she was still searching for the words to comfort me while thinking, *What the hell are you talking about?* You're probably wondering the same thing. Yes, Momma was my grandmother. And my mother? Well, that's a whole 'nother story. In fact, it's *the* story. I know it's all a bit confusing right now, so I won't leave you hanging. How about I tell it from the very beginning? But you better be ready for a wild ride.... Get yourself a glass of whatever you like to drink and sit yo ass down. This shit's going to make the Twilight Zone look like Disneyland. And don't worry, we'll get back to this *Empire* night soon enough....

chapter 2

Candy

Buffalo, New York. Known for its Buffalo wings, heavy winter snowfalls, the infamous fruit belt and, most of all, the Buffalo Bills. Back in the mid-nineties, the Bills were led by a hardworking quarterback named Jim Kelly, who was instrumental in taking the team all the way to the Super Bowl four times in a row. It was also during the sixties, seventies, and early eighties that Buffalo's economy boomed, centering on thriving factories like Bethlehem Steel and major tourist attractions like Niagara Falls.

I grew up on the East Side of Buffalo. The East Side of Buffalo, like most other east sides, was mainly populated by black folks, and for the most part was pretty cool and moderately safe. Most neighborhoods were livable, but far from the kept lawns and swimming pool-filled yards of the surrounding suburbs, like Cheektowaga. One particular mid-July summer day on Guilford Street, like most Buffalo summers, the heat beat down so hard it seemed to melt the asphalt. Down on the corner somebody had turned on the fire hydrant, and all the neighborhood kids were playing and running through the water to cool off. Even some adults took the opportunity to rinse off the heat of the day. This would go on until the scorching sun began to set, or until the fire department came to shut off the makeshift waterpark, whichever came first. Just a regular summer day of fooling around.

Stuck on the porch of 58 Guilford playing with her dolls was a chunky nine-year-old girl who had the skin of a dark chocolate bar and a spirit as pure as an angel's. Her jet-black, shoulder-length hair was pressed straight and held down by two over-sized pink barrettes. Lela, or "Candy" as she was appropriately nicknamed by her mother, was a good-natured child with a smile that could light up a thousand rooms. She was as happy as could be, playing all alone with her dolls while humming songs and nursery rhymes, completely lost in her own world. The thing about Candy, though, was that she wasn't like the other children in the neighborhood, and those who were around her never gave her a chance to forget it.

"I'm gonna beat yo butt," Candy scolded one of her dolls as she hobbled along on a crudely crafted wooden leg down toward the other side of the porch. Before she arrived, she started to hear the familiar voices from down the sidewalk:

"Hey, there, one-legged freak!"

"Handicapped little bitch!"

"Look at the retard over there."

"Hey, Candy, wanna hit some baseballs with that leg you got?"

They all burst out laughing.

Candy looked back at them with her innocent eyes, and even though she didn't understand everything they were saying, she could feel that they were being mean. I'm sure that in her own naive way she wondered how they could be so cruel and wished they liked her instead. Her thoughts were interrupted with more hurtful words.

"Hey, No-Leg."

"Little Miss Pissy...still wearing your diaper at nine years old!"

"Why you all messed up?"

Defenseless, Candy tried to speak up for herself, saying in a soft voice, "Leave me alone, stop saying those things." She fought back her tears and hoped they would do what she said, but they didn't, and they never would, they were simply joined by the laughing voices of more children returning home from their day of fun.

"My momma said don't touch her."

"Yeah, she a one-legged monster."

"She can't walk right, and if she touches my leg, she gonna give it to me!"

Candy sat silently in the middle of the porch as they mocked her, unable to stop the tears streaming down her face. She closed her eyes and wiped it away, knowing more would soon follow.

The raggedy old wooden screen door flung open and a raging voice yelled, "Get the hell outta here before I whip all y'all sorry asses!" The firecracker of a woman ran to the edge of the porch and the kids scattered like cockroaches when the light goes on. This was one woman the neighborhood kids, and some of the adults, didn't want to have a run-in with. Known by her sixteen brothers and sisters as Ida Mae, she preferred to be called one or the other. Ida, when she was being sophisticated or dealing with white folks, Mae when she was being a bitch or around family and friends. Mae was Candy's mother and, for the most part, her protector.

Because of Candy's condition, Mae was used to people mistreating or teasing her, so she was always within arms' reach wherever Candy was. She'd be the first to tell you that it wasn't easy, but a mother gotta do what a mother gotta do, and Candy was her baby girl.

She looked at her momma with tears in her eyes. "Those kids don't like me, and I don't know what I did to make them say those mean things to me."

To put it mildly, Mae always had a way with words, and looking back, I realized this was her way of showing strength. "Girl, you didn't do shit, so don't you worry about them lil bad-ass kids! They ain't got no sense no way!" She led Candy back into the house. When she slammed the door, the broken latch on the old screen door clicked behind them.

Once they were inside, Candy cradled her dolls and went over to the couch to play while Mae disappeared into the kitchen. Moments later, she heard dishes clanking and cupboards being slammed around. Candy could hear Mae muttering things under her breath that she couldn't make out one minute, then yelling at the top of her voice the next. Candy never heard her momma like this before, but truth be told, Mae was in there taking her anger out on anything in sight.

Tears welled up in her eyes. Mae knew that something had to give, that she was not going to do it on her own like she thought she could after her last relationship broke down. She needed someone, and it better be someone good and reliable. A man came to her mind, and she suddenly stopped her ranting and calmed herself down.

Mae came out of the kitchen with a tray in her hands. On it was some food for Candy and a glass of water, and next to that, a bunch of different colored pills. Mae set down the tray and turned on the TV. "Take all them pills before you eat, Candy baby," she said sweetly before disappearing into her bedroom.

Candy did as she was told, even though she had an uneasy feeling that she done something wrong, as usual. But with the TV on, food to eat, and her dolls to play with, she was distracted from her thoughts for a time, and as evening transitioned into the silence of many nights and the cars that had been passing finally slowed down, Candy started to wonder what had happened to her mother and why she wasn't coming out of her bedroom. She got up and went and opened Mae's door a crack.

"Momma?" Mae was wriggling into her tightest skirt, already wearing her longest hair and highest heels. She'd spent the last hour making herself prettier than Candy had ever seen her momma look, and Candy smiled. "You're so pretty, Momma. Where are you going?"

"Out!" Then she called her son, who was playing in the backyard. "Peewee!" then seconds later, "Peewee!" Peewee came running in the back door and Mae whopped him on the back of his head. "Where the hell were you and what were you doin'? I've been calling yo ass for hours. Now you take care of Candy, and I'll see y'all in the morning." She checked her face in the mirror once more and, satisfied, grabbed her bag and left the room.

Candy watched her walk to the front door and, when the rickety old screen door slammed shut behind her, off she went.

A preoccupied guy and small for his age, Peewee took care of Candy as best he could when Mae wasn't around, which was most every night. Wondering why Mae took off earlier than usual bugged him a lot because she'd never gone out before Candy was asleep. He tried not to show his feelings, and after fixing himself something to eat and watching some TV with his younger sister, Peewee got Candy into bed. He then went straight into his room and took the ripped-out pages of an old X-rated magazine that he'd stolen out from under his bed where he had stashed a ton of the stuff.

With almost everyone settling down a bit, if you listened close enough, even through the stillness of the night, you could hear and feel the undertones of sadness, stress, unfaithfulness, disregard, and abuse that hung thick in the air, just like the heat of that particular Buffalo summer.

chapter 3

Hooked

The music was loud, the energy high, and the drinks were flowing. Hooks, the neighborhood bar, was open most days and every single night. Unlike *Cheers*, where everybody knows your name, if you were a regular at Hooks, everyone knew not only your name but your social security number, your momma's name, and *her* social security number. Men buying drinks and doing their best to impress was normal, and tonight was no exception. Remember, it was summer and humid, so asses were out, charging the air with a whole lot of highly charged sexual energy.

Mae and her crew were regulars at Hooks. Not only a good-looking woman, she wasn't at all shy, and was certainly no stranger with the men. You didn't get three kids with three different men if talking to the opposite sex was an issue. Married, single, it didn't matter. If Mae set her mind on one, he was as good as hers, even if it was only for a night or two. This made her popular with the fellas and less favorable with the other women. Not that she cared what they thought. It wasn't like she didn't want someone permanent, she did, but her experience up until then hadn't been all that great, and the life she had right now was proof of that. The fact was, Mae was no easy woman to get along with, and her home life wasn't exactly *Little House on the Prairie.*

However, tonight she had this crazy feeling that the man she had her sights on wouldn't care about any of that, that he would be able to take care of her proper, her and her kids. That made the shit easier to deal with. After Candy was born and her father took off like the rest of them, she went on a sexual rampage. Now she was ready for all that to stop, and she was convinced that her only way out was gonna be a man with money. She knew exactly who that man was. She'd seen him in there a bunch of times, but the competition had always been too thick, and by the time she'd arrive, which was usually far later, he'd already be on his way out with at least one gal hanging on his arm. Tonight The Catch would be hers, she promised herself.

Alton Burder was his name, and for Jabo, the nickname he was called by everyone he knew, it looked like a night like any other. Sitting in the corner at his regular spot with a good view of all the happenings on the dance floor, he could talk with his friends while keeping an eye on any woman he'd not had before. Yeah, Jabo was a hardworking factory worker by day, and by night, he was the kind of man whose pants were always pressed, his shoes shined, his hat tilted to one side on his handsome head, and his wallet wide open. He was famously known by the women as "The Catch" and a complete and total ladies' man by his buddies.

Jabo owned cars and homes and didn't mind flashing his money and spending it. Like Mae with the menfolk, Jabo was very popular with the ladies. He would pick them up, try them on, wear them for a night, and never talk to them again, even if they came by his table, cursing at him while sticking their cleavage in his face. Jabo knew his power, and some say the man would even glide when he walked. He was the type of guy who made other men insecure before he even walked into the room. Jabo never really settled with any woman for an extended period of time, they just didn't keep his interest. Or if they did, it was easily swayed by another. But he also was getting tired of that life and would sometimes say, "I am gettin' way too old for this shit." The problem was, how was he gonna find the right lady without getting bored with her within twelve hours?

He didn't know it then, but this question would be answered soon, since this was going to be a very different night for both him and Mae.

When Mae arrived, she spotted Jabo over in his favorite corner surrounded by his less-cool buddies and a fan of women. Although she pretended like she hadn't seen him, she kept him in clear view while he was laughing loud and taking shots. Then he sent a message up to the owner and bartender, Big Mary, to play his favorite song, "The Thrill is Gone" by B.B. King, right when Mae was walking up to the bar to see who was going to buy her a drink. Since Jabo was a regular, and considered friends with Big Mary and her husband John D., Mary yelled out, "You don't run nothing 'round here, Jabo, but I'mma put it on this one time, but not next!"

Everybody laughed, knowing their relationship. As long as Jabo kept spending money, Big Mary would play every damn one of his favorites.

The opening bars of the song began and Jabo jumped up out of his seat. "Yeah, baby, that's my song!"

Mae downed her drink, and before the first guitar lick began, she raised her arms and yelled, "Oh, yes, I *love* me some B.B. King!" She started dancing and snapping her fingers, moving her hips so hard you would've thought she was gonna knock one of them out of place.

Jabo noticed Mae straight through his entourage, this woman he had seen before but had never talked to. Tonight there was something about the way she moved, something that caught his eye so that he couldn't take his gaze off her. Jabo was definitely impressed.

Mae turned him on, and she knew it. Even from across the room she could feel the sex-tricity. Big Mary went over to Jabo's table and set down another drink, then smiled as she watched Jabo's gaze follow the sexy hip and pelvic thrusts.

"Watch out Jabo, I don't think even *you* can handle that," Big Mary said, laughing loud as she went back to the bar to keep the drinks flowing.

Jabo got out of his seat and went over to the table where Mae was dancing. He held out his hand to her. "The name's Alton."

"I know who you are...Jabo," Mae said, not taking his hand, and definitely not stopping her dance.

"Oh, you know me, do you?" Jabo casually slipped his hands back into his pants pockets. The game was on.

"Of course I do. Every woman on the East Side of Buffalo knows Mister Alton Burder."

Jabo laughed without taking his eyes off the prize. "Maybe they *think* they know him, but...how would you like to get to know him better?" He wasn't asking.

Mae slowly lowered her arms as Jabo came in closer and began to put his hands around her waist. She placed a hand on his chest and pushed him away gently, "You know, Mister Jabo, I'm not like any of those other women you can just say a few words to and make 'em fall into your arms, so—"

Before she could say any more, he kissed her, and she fell right into his arms.

When the song stopped playing and they were still kissing, everybody in the bar stood and watched, both the gals and the guys, equally pissed, pleased, or disappointed, wanting one or both of them for themselves. Everyone in the bar started cheering and laughing.

"Aww, another Hooks love connection," said Big Mary. "Let's see how long this one lasts," she added with a smirk as she put on the next record.

Jabo winked at Big Mary then led Mae in another dance while the crowd got back to their business. The night wore on and the two danced and drank the hours away until everyone had left and it was just the two of them sitting at Jabo's corner table.

Big Mary and John D. were cleaning up the bar, and Big Mary asked as she walked by, "Y'all want some coffee?"

"I'll have a cup, that'd be nice. You want one too?" Jabo asked Mae sweetly. Mae declined. She still had the taste of alcohol on her lips and she wasn't ready to change that. "So, Miss Mae, tell me about yourself."

Mae wasn't used to talking about herself to men, they usually got right down to it, which was one of the clues she had that this was going to be different. She needed to play it well if she was gonna keep this one. She decided to lay her cards, well...most of them, right down on the table.

"I'm thirty-six and originally from Mississippi. I got three kids, two boys, my oldest is in the Army, and my daughter, she's a very special child. Oh, and I'm one of sixteen brothers and sisters, so in case you fixing to try some funny stuff..."

Jabo laughed, but he knew the threat was real. You didn't go messing with *anyone* who had that kind of backup. "What do you mean by special?" he asked, genuinely curious about her little girl.

"My daughter, I call her Candy 'cause she so sweet, but her actual name is Lela—anyway, she was born with a deformity in one of her legs and they had to amputate it when she was born. Also, her kidneys and other organs never fully developed so she has medical issues. Nobody really knows what's going on inside that child's body. She has to take a bunch of pills every day, and honestly, Jabo, I don't know how long we gonna have her with us. She's a nine-year-old, but sometimes it feels like she hasn't changed since she was about three. Kind of a slow learner, you know? Doctors told me it's 'cause we baby her. But she's my baby," Mae said with a smile. "I do my best to protect her and make sure that whatever time she has left is good."

Jabo laid a sympathetic hand on Mae's arm and gave her a sweet kiss, like he understood everything she was going through. She was hooked, giving the bar full credit to its name.

"Look at me, I'm talking your ear off," she said. "Tell me about you."

"Me? I have a daughter too, who's thirty-three, and a seven-teen-year-old grandson. I work at Bethlehem Steel, but I'm retiring this year, and I plan to travel and relax for the rest of my life 'cause I've definitely earned it." Mae smiled at him. "What's wrong?"

"Nothing. It's just that I never saw you as someone other than a ladies' man who I'd see here on occasion. I guess the thought never crossed my head that you and I would even talk, much less anything else."

Jabo kissed her again, this time longer, then said, "Mae, I think there's a reason you came into my life right now. To be honest with you, I'm getting too old to keep playing the field. Not to mention the fact that I've already plowed just about everyone in it." Mae let out a loud laugh. "You seem like a good woman. Hell, you must be 'cause you even laugh at my jokes."

This was music to Mae's ears, and if she wasn't dreaming, she might actually have just caught the biggest fish on the East Side of Buffalo. She liked that Jabo was tall, dark, and handsome. But most of all *rich*, which was pretty much what sealed the deal for her. Then he surprised her with something she'd never expected to hear in a million years.

"Mae, I want to invite you and your kids over for dinner on Tuesday if you don't have any plans."

Mae almost fell off her chair but managed to keep her cool. She smiled. "Jabo, I'd like that very much."

They kissed again until Big Mary's booming voice came at them from behind the bar.

"Okay, you two lovebirds. It's five forty-five in the morning and y'all ain't gotta go home, but you *do* gotta get the hell outta my bar!"

Jabo took the last sip of coffee and they both stood up.

"Come on, let me take you home." Jabo kissed Big Mary on the cheek, slapped John D. on the back, and escorted Mae outside into the dawn of the day.

"For some reason, I got a feeling them two just might work," Big Mary said to John D. She turned off the lights and closed the back door to the bar.

John D. looked up at Big Mary and said real slow, "Shiiiiiiiit!"

chapter 4

Church Fight

Mae showed up late to the Sunday morning service after a night with Jabo, just as high as the spirits at Mt. Carmel Baptist Church. Mt. Carmel was the place where the Monday through Saturday night sinners would come and show off their outfits, gossip, look for husbands (even if they already had one), and for maybe an hour or two of holiness. Mae was no different. Except for today. This was the last time she'd come to church a sinner because now she had a man. And what a man. She smiled to herself at the thought of them all falling off their chairs the first time she walked in with him to the next church service. They'd react just like she had when he asked her to dinner with him and his family. I mean, who asks a lady they just met to bring her family along and meet his unless he's serious about her?

When Mae came in through the side door of the church, the choir was beginning its march into the sanctuary. You could hear every tambourine two blocks away. One of the ushers helped Mae and Candy to the only available seats, and she blew a kiss to her mother, Mrs. Lula

L. Spencer, who we all knew as Granny. After cutting her eyes at Mae for coming in late, Granny rocked from side to side to the music along with the rest of the mothers in the front row, who were known as The Mothers' Board. Mae's face went from a cocky smile to a frown when she saw who she was being seated next to.

Nancy Johnson was the longtime girlfriend of a man everyone knew as Windy. He was known as being a very kind man, but Windy was a bad-looking version of Gregory Hines. Rumor had it that he and Mae were fooling around behind Nancy's back, which was completely true, and by the look on Nancy's face, Mae could tell that Nancy knew it too. Avoiding Nancy's dagger eyes at all costs, Mae sat down and got herself and Candy situated. If looks could kill, this celebration would have been Mae's funeral instead of a Sunday service. Nancy turned her lips down and held her head up.

Hand clapping and foot stomping rang out all over the building. The choir went to the vamp of the song and the church erupted with almost everyone in the building catching the Holy Ghost. Having almost forgotten about Nancy and Windy and the shitty things she'd done, Mae felt the warmth of the spirit heating up inside her. Hanging onto every word pastor Reverend Miller said, she waved her hands and yelled, "Yes, Lord!"

And as the song ended and the musicians were finalizing their musical frenzy with a rumbling of instruments, Nancy caught what she wanted everyone to believe was the Holy Ghost too, and started flinging her arms faster and faster, yelling, "Yes, Lord!" and "Thank ya, Jesus!" Then, out of nowhere, she cold punched Mae straight in the face.

Mae's glasses went to the left and her head to the right. Thankfully, the whole thing happened so fast no one actually saw it, and when she opened her eyes, an usher was standing in front of her with a tissue, thinking she was also in the spirit. When Mae raised her face up to thank him, she found herself staring into the face of Isaphene, Nancy's younger sister, who had a look like she was going to kill her. Mae grabbed the tissue, stood up, and hoping no one would notice while things were still in the thick, grabbed Candy and darted out the doors they'd come in through.

Mae pulled out of the church parking lot and cried all the way home. Candy had no idea what was going on and started crying too, but Mae was so embarrassed by what had happened she ignored her. Burning up with humiliation, even though it wasn't the first time something like this had happened, she was sure as hell determined that it would be the last. Now, more than ever, she was going to have to make her relationship with Jabo be her last so that all of those women would have something else to talk about and she'd never be in that position again.

chapter 5

The Birthday Party,
Part One

"Candy, hold still or I'm gonna burn yo face," Mae said as she flattened Candy's hair with a curling iron, getting the last kinks out before finishing it off with her favorite barrettes. The kitchen smelled like fried hair and smoke.

"Momma, that hurts!" Candy cried.

"Why now all of a sudden? Don't I do this every damn week?"

Candy knew not to contradict Momma when she was hell-bent on doing something, but she'd never ironed her hair with this much force, that was for sure. "I'm sorry, Momma."

"I just want everything to be perfect, baby girl. We gotta make a good impression."

"Good impression on who, Momma?" Peewee asked as he came running into the kitchen.

"Peewee, I told you we was going over to Mister Burder's for dinner tonight," Mae said impatiently, "so take off those pants and go and get your good pair of jeans."

20

"Okay, Momma." Peewee knew not to make her angry, and for some reason today she seemed extra tense.

Mae was more than nervous about meeting Jabo's family. They'd only known each other a couple of days and already they were going to meet each other's family. It was such a clear positive sign, she for sure didn't want to blow her chance. She would no longer be known as the party girl with a few kids who was going nowhere.

Knowing Momma, she probably thought, *I'm finally gonna be somebody, I'm going somewhere, and things are going to change. I hope these damn kids act right!*

"Ouch!" Candy yelped again when the curling iron touched her face.

"Girl, if you'd sit still then you won't get burnt!" Mae scolded.

Candy, confused since she'd been sitting there as still as if she had been asleep, looked up at Mae and smiled as sweet as she could to get back on her good side, but Mae's mind was elsewhere...as usual.

They finally made it out of the house and took the bus down to a slightly better part of town where Mae had only dreamt of living. Candy looked just like her name, wearing a pink dress and one white patent leather shoe on her foot. Peewee was entertaining his little sister with a magic trick he'd learned with some cards, but the cards kept falling on the floor of the bus, which didn't do anything but get on Mae's nerves.

"Peewee, pick them damn cards back up and stop fidgeting!" Mae barked at the boy.

"Yes, Momma." He put them back in his pocket. He had planned to show Mr. Burder the trick.

The three of them sat in silence while the bus made the short trip to Jabo's house.

* * *

Bernice, Jabo's only daughter, who everyone called Bonnie, was six foot one, as loud as she was tall, and had a sense of humor to match her height. She was also very much Daddy's girl, and therefore fiercely protective of him. She was in the kitchen preparing some mac and cheese while her son Kevin stood looking out the window, admiring the car Jabo had bought him. Kevin was Jabo's only grandson, so he was as spoiled as spoiled could be. They were close, almost as close as a father and son, and Kevin called Jabo "Daddy."

Jabo was coming out of the back room when the front door flung open. "I know you didn't get that boy no Porsche, Jabo."

Jabo had a guilty look on his face.

"Lord have mercy, he only seventeen years old. Why don't you just go get him a jet?" She handed Jabo a big box covered in elaborate wrapping paper. "This is for *you*."

"Oda-Lee, now don't you come in here messing with me on my birthday," Jabo said playfully. "I got all I need, so let the boy have some fun." He put the box down and gave his younger sister Oda-Lee a big hug.

Oda-Lee was called Anie by the young folks and was the one in the family who said all the things everyone else wanted to say but didn't have the nerve to. Her daughter Betty came in behind her. Betty was twenty-one and an only child. Oda-Lee released herself from Jabo's arms and went over to the kitchen area.

"Is the turkey done yet? I don't know if I want no turkey Bonnie cooked anyway!"

"I followed all the instructions you gave me," Bonnie said while grating cheese and rinsing off the macaroni.

"I know you did, and last time you followed directions the dog ended up dead. You always finds a way, child." Oda-Lee shook her head, and everybody started laughing. Except Bonnie. "Betty, you and Kevin go set the table. I think we gonna be ten, and I'll take over the cooking, make sure it's seasoned right."

Betty and Kevin did as they were told, and Jabo went over to his two work buddies who were sitting on the couch shooting the shit.

When the two of them were alone in the kitchen area, Oda-Lee started looking for her favorite seasoning salt and putting the final touches on dinner.

Bonnie leaned up against the counter and folded her arms across her chest. "Anie, can I talk to you about something?"

"Girl, if it's about that comment I just made, you know I'm joking with ya," she said with a smile, knowing she wasn't.

"No, Anie, it's not that, it's something else."

Oda-Lee stopped what she was doing and looked straight at Bonnie. "You know you can ask me anything. What's wrong, baby?"

* * *

Peewee let out a low whistle as they approached Jabo's house. "Nice place."

Mae raised an eyebrow and frowned at him, but a slight smile did cross her lips, thinking how right he was. She was already packing boxes in her mind.

They approached the steps going up to the house, and Mae made sure one more time that her kids weren't gonna be the reason she and Jabo wouldn't work out. "You two better be on your best behavior, you hear me? I will whoop both your asses if you do anything stupid." With the fear of God firmly in place, they walked up to the house, Mae holding onto Candy's arm while she limped up the steps. They could hear laughter coming from inside the house as well as the sounds of Bobby "Blue" Bland playing.

Her heart beating faster and her palms clammy, Mae rang the doorbell.

In the kitchen, Bonnie was just about to tell Oda-Lee what was on her mind, but the doorbell interrupted her. Jabo got up and went to the door himself, Bonnie following close behind. No sense telling Oda-Lee what she'd be seeing for herself in a few minutes.

Kevin grinned at Betty. "Daddy never gets the door."

Jabo swung it open and smiled when he saw Mae and her children standing there. Right behind him, Bonnie frowned when she saw 'that woman' and her two kids looking so dressed up she thought they'd got the days mixed up and were on their way to church. Knowing exactly who Ida Mae was, her blood started to boil. This was not the lady she envisioned for her precious daddy to settle down with.

"Mae! Come on in. Come on, Mae!" Jabo excitedly reached out his hand to pull her inside. Bonnie moved out of the way and slinked back into the kitchen. Jabo took Candy's hand and bent down to her level. "You must be Candy. It is so nice to meet you."

Candy flashed her million-dollar smile and stepped up into the house. Then it was Peewee's turn. The men shook hands and Jabo closed the door behind them.

Mae and her kids stood looking around the living room awkwardly. A couple of men were sitting on the couch who looked like they might be friends of Jabo's from work. On the other side of the room there was a large dining table and beyond that, an open kitchen. There were balloons everywhere and a banner over the fireplace that read *Happy Birthday, Jabo*.

Mae's heart jumped into her throat. *Oh my God. It's his birthday.*

Jabo didn't give her more time to think about it. Excited, he took her by the hand and pulled her to him, giving Mae the biggest hug. "Welcome to my home, baby," he said, then kissed her.

She kissed him back, forgetting for just a minute they were surrounded by people, then said, "Happy birthday, sneaky," giving him a playful swat on the arm for not telling her. They exchanged loving looks then Jabo turned his attention to his guests. "Hey, everybody, I want y'all to meet Ida Mae Spencer and her kids, Candy and Peewee. She likes to be called Mae and just in case you don't know, Mae is my girlfriend, so you better treat her right." Everybody was smiling and introducing themselves, except for Anie, who was still over in the kitchen tending to the food and making sure it was edible, and Bonnie. Mae almost felt completely overwhelmed by everyone coming to her at once. Well, almost everyone.

"No present?" Bonnie said, her arms crossed.

Mae was so mortified she would have liked to crawl underneath the coffee table, but Jabo protectively put his arm around her, letting Bonnie and everyone else know where his loyalties were now going to be lying. "I didn't tell Mae it was my birthday on purpose. Now let's all sit down and have a nice dinner. It's my day so I don't want no lip from any of y'all." He ended his speech with a look at his daughter as they all headed over to the table. Bonnie walked off in a huff.

"This dressin' is gonna be the talk of the dinner, I put my own personal touch on it!" Oda-Lee bragged, setting the platter of turkey and stuffing on the table.

"Mae," said Jabo, "I want you to meet my sister, Oda-Lee."

"Hello, Mae, nice to meet you, shuga," Oda-Lee said, and meant it.

"Nice to meet you too, Miss Oda-Lee."

"Girl, just call me Oda-Lee. Hell, I ain't that old. And who is this cute little black girl? And where is her other leg?" Oda-Lee said with concern.

"That's my daughter Candy. She was born with a bad leg that had to be amputated at birth." Mae and the children sat down at the table. "And this is my son Peewee."

"She looks just as sweet as her name. And why Peewee? Where did you get *that* from? He look like a normal-sized boy to me!" Oda-Lee gave Peewee a wink.

"He was born premature and had to stay in the hospital almost three months," Mae explained.

Oda-Lee gave Peewee a pat on the head and started off toward the kitchen. "I got all the information I need. Now, Mae, you come on in this kitchen and help us bring out the food for these hungry men."

Mae liked Oda-Lee right away and was happy to go and help with whatever she needed. The ladies entered the kitchen. "Mae, you met my niece, Bonnie...." Oda-Lee glanced around the kitchen, but Bonnie was nowhere to be found. "Oh, I'm sorry, I don't know where she went. She'll show up once we got the food out." The last plates were finally brought to the table, and everyone sat down for Jabo's birthday dinner. Ten people in all, almost everyone in good spirits.

"Let's all bow our heads and take the person's hand next to you and say grace," Jabo began. Heads were bowed and hands held. "Lord, thank you for another year on this blessed planet and thank you for

the friends and family members that you have gathered here today...."
He stole a glance at Mae, who returned the look. "I want to also thank
you for your abundance in the food we are about to eat. Everyone,
please feel welcome at this table..."

"Almost everyone," Bonnie said under her breath. Betty looked
over at Bonnie in disbelief, the only one to have heard Bonnie's insult
clearly.

"...and as a family," Jabo continued. "Our road is long and sometimes feels hard, but Jesus is always there for us if we are there
for each other. Please be with us to remind us that the way will be
easier, amen."

Everyone lifted their heads and were just about to dig into the
food when Bonnie couldn't keep her mouth shut any longer.

She looked directly at Mae. "Yes, it sho can get a lot easier if you
the neighborhood ho looking for a way out and you nab yourself an
older man with money."

Jabo looked up at his daughter, fire in his eyes.

"Girl, are you crazy?" Oda-Lee asked.

"No, Anie, I'm not crazy, but Daddy must be if he thinks this family
wants that trash to be a part of it!"

"Bonnie, don't you sit here and disrespect me at this table!" Jabo
shouted, slamming a fist on the table.

"Fine," said Bonnie. She jumped up so fast her plate turned over
and ran to the back of the house.

"Go on, get the hell outta here, then!" Jabo shouted after her.

Oda-Lee leaned over and said to Betty, "Lordy, lord, this why I
stopped coming over as much as I used to."

Mae sat there looking uncomfortable. She couldn't completely
deny what Bonnie said, but she was in love with Jabo and his money
or his looks didn't change any of that. Not completely....

"I'm sorry for my daughter, everyone. Mae, honey, are you okay?"

"I'm fine, Jabo." Mae gave him the sweetest smile that would have
melted his heart, if it weren't melted already.

The guests got back to the business of eating and making small talk, all of them trying to move past the uncomfortable moment. Knowing how Mae must have felt getting welcomed like that, they were all overly nice to her and the two children. After dinner everyone sat around laughing, drinking, and telling stories.

"She would wait right good until Momma would leave and then she would bust those biscuits open and put butter and sugar in them," Oda-Lee said. "That's when Jabo would come to my rescue and say 'leave me and my sister alone. We don't want that mess, ole cotton-eyed Joe,'" Oda-Lee continued while laughing. "That was our grandmother doing that mess to us. She was just evil, wasn't she, Jabo?"

"Yeah, she most certainly was. She wore them old high-necked dresses to cover this huge goiter she had on her neck," he said. "We thought it would kill her, and hell, we hoped it would!"

"Did it, Daddy?" Kevin asked.

"Hell naw. That old goat lived to be one hundred and four years old. She outlived all her children," Jabo said and Oda-Lee laughed like it was the first time she'd heard that story.

This went on about three more hours until finally the guests started to leave. Mae decided it was about time they got going too, even though Candy was on the couch and Peewee curled up in the chair, both of them fast asleep. "Jabo, I think it's about time for me to take them home."

"It feels to me like they already are home," Jabo said softly. "Doesn't it feel like that to you, Mae?"

"I can't say it does. Bonnie made sure of that."

"I'm sorry about Bonnie, but believe me, she will be fine. Anyway, this is my house and so is the one she and Kevin live in next door." Jabo gave Mae a kiss. "Why don't you all stay here tonight? Hm? It's my birthday, and Bonnie was right about one thing...you didn't bring me a present."

This was exactly what she wanted, but for a brief moment Mae thought about the things Bonnie had said and she wasn't sure. Yet there was something in his eyes that was undeniable.

"I hate the thought of waking up my babies," she said. "The buses aren't running this late, and…"

"And?" Jabo prompted when Mae stopped talking for a second.

"And it's your birthday and I owe you that present." They both started laughing.

"Good. Now I gotta put they asses out so I can spend time with you." Jabo went into the living room to dismiss the last of the guests, including Kevin, who lived next door with his mother.

Jabo and Mae put Candy and Peewee in the two spare bedrooms and settled into the reclining chair together. He put his arms around her and thanked her for a wonderful birthday. Jabo was so content having her in his arms, away from everyone. He was sure Mae was finally the right one for him, and from the look in his eyes, she knew it too. And of course, she felt the same way.

"Be careful, birthday boy, because I could get used to this."

"I could too." Jabo got up, turned off the lights, and led Mae into his bedroom.

chapter 6

A New Start

The rosebush in front of Jabo's house was in full bloom. The beautiful red blossoms started at the foundation and went far past the roof of the house. A gorgeous black and orange monarch butterfly landed on one of the larger roses, punctuated by the chirping of sparrows. The scene was idyllic. The guests stood there, lined up on either side of the stairs, waiting for the couple to come out of the house.

"Congratulations, big brother," Oda-Lee said, tossing a small fistful of rice over Jabo's head.

Jabo grinned. "I'm gon' get you after this."

Everyone cheered and congratulated the newlyweds.

"What a lovely couple," someone said. And they were.

"How long they known each other? A month?" another guest was heard to say. "Lord have mercy!"

Still, everyone could see that Mr. and Mrs. Burder were a happy couple and they blessed them with their good wishes and smiles.

The only person who *didn't* smile was Bonnie. In fact, she was standing at the far end of the porch with tears in her eyes. When she couldn't take it anymore, she stormed off down the stairs, right behind Mae and Jabo, almost knocking Mae down in her beautiful white dress. "Daddy, you don't even know this bitch," she spat as she passed.

Climbing the stairs to the porch of her house next door, Bonnie yelled, "She'll never take the place of my momma and I'll never accept that bitch in this family."

Kevin ran after her. Bonnie always said that if there were two people in this world who would be there for her forever, it was Kevin and her father. Now that Mae was in the picture, this was a direct threat to Bonnie.

"I'm not going to just sit back and let that gold-digging tramp come in here and destroy my family," she said to Kevin. "I will never let that happen. I didn't let it happen with the others, and I sure as shit won't let it happen with this low-life bitch."

Bonnie went in the house with Kevin following close behind.

Once inside, Kevin went to the window. The horn blew on Jabo's car and he and Mae drove off down the street, tin cans attached to the bumper with fishing wire dragging behind them. "Just Married" was written in big letters with shaving cream on the back window for the entire neighborhood to see. Kevin knew where *his* loyalties were, and he decided he would do whatever it took to protect his mother.

Before the wedding, movers had packed up Mae's belongings and taken them to Jabo's house. Mae didn't even know how to act because last time she moved, they used somebody's pickup truck and got some of the neighborhood teenagers to help. Jabo had already started taking care of his bride. She didn't have to worry about the kids since Granny would be taking care of Candy while Mae and Jabo went to Niagara Falls for a honeymoon get away.

If you'll recall, Granny had sixteen children, and almost all of them had kids of their own, so Granny was working full time taking care of one or the other. This meant she had no time to be dealing with any of Mae's dramas, of which there had been plenty to choose from over the years. In fact, at one point she said to Mae, "I love you like I love

30

all my children, and I love Candy and Peewee, but you don't make the best choices. I ain't got time to be playing Dear Abby with you, so I'll make you a deal. I'll help you out when I can and if I think the reason is a good one, otherwise you are on your own." Evidently, she thought a honeymoon was a good reason and so she took the time to stay while Mae and Jabo were away.

All throughout their trip, Mae couldn't believe her dream of having a happy family had come true. Everyone around them gave her the feeling that their marriage could not have been more perfect...apart from Bonnie. If anything was going to tear them apart it would be Bonnie's attitude, and Mae wanted to talk to him about her fears, to make their honeymoon the beginning of a fresh start, even though part of her didn't want to ruin it with talking about Bonnie. But she knew she would have to for her own sanity. Mae hoped the opportunity would arise without her having to push it, and to her surprise, it did.

They were having breakfast one morning at a local diner, all hugged up in a corner booth, when Mae told Jabo how she was feeling. "Jabo, I never thought I would be this happy, I swear to you on my life. Up until now it's been one bullshit struggle after the other and now, I still can't believe I've met the love of my life."

"You better believe it, babe. The minute I saw you, I knew I was done with my old ways." He took her face in his hands. "You are my favorite girl, and don't you ever forget that."

"Favorite girl? Oh, lord, don't you ever let Bonnie hear you say that. She would cut off my head."

Somehow Jabo knew this was coming too, and decided it would be best they get it all out in the open now so that when they got home, it wouldn't be an issue anymore. That was his hope, anyway. "Bonnie is just spoiled," he said. "She really likes you, I know she does, she just doesn't see me with anyone except her mother and she never has."

Mae knew about Bonnie's mother Mary. She was one of the most beautiful redbone women you ever wanted to see, and she and Jabo were an item when they were in their twenties and thirties. But, just like his father, grandfather, and great-grandfather before him, none of the men were the type to stay in one place for long and certainly not able to stay with one woman for any period of time.

"I don't know if that's the only reason, Jabo. You saw the way she talked to me on your birthday, calling me a ho in front of all them people. It's pretty damn obvious she doesn't think I'm good enough for you."

Jabo started to protest, but deep down, he knew she was right.

"So many times she's looking at me like she could kill me, then smiles when you come in the room. It makes things so uncomfortable when I'm in the house alone with her. Or anywhere alone with her for that matter."

"Mae, listen, baby. I know Bonnie can be a bit of a bully, but you are my wife and I love you. Nothing is going to change that. I will do everything I can to protect you, I promise."

Just then the waitress came up asked if they wanted anything to drink. "Coffee, please," they said at the same time, then started to laugh.

"Just like an old married couple," Jabo said as the waitress went off. "Anyway, I think maybe the shock of knowing I'm finally settled down hasn't set in for Bonnie yet, but it won't take long."

"Yeah, maybe you're right. One or two ain't too long."

Jabo gave her a confused look. "One or two...?"

"Million years," Mae said sarcastically and Jabo laughed and gave her a kiss.

The waitress came back with the coffee and set the mugs in front of them.

"It won't be that long, babe, I promise." He opened two packs of sugar and put them in his coffee then reached for another two.

Mae put a hand on his and smiled. "That's enough sugar, Sugar, remember what the doctor said, you have to be careful with your diabetes."

"I feel fine. Besides, who the hell likes bitter, black-ass coffee? Who the hell likes *anything* bitter?"

"I know, but Dr. Wright said you needed to be a bit more careful."

"I'm careful." Jabo stirred the next two packets into his cup. "Now let's carefully get our asses up and get some of that damn food before I starve to death."

Charmed as usual, Mae just smiled and the two of them slipped out of the booth and walked over to the buffet.

chapter 7

Night Crawler

Today was the day Peewee and Candy would leave their old home and move into their new one for good. When Granny, Peewee, and Candy pulled up in front of the house with the last of their belongings a few days before Mae and Jabo's return from their honeymoon, Bonnie and Kevin were standing on the porch next door watching them.

"Not only is she a ho, she's bringing her retarded kids with her. I hear she got an older boy too. Wonder what the hell's wrong with that one," Bonnie said to Kevin as Candy made her difficult way up the steps.

"I think he's in the Army, Ma," Kevin said, trying to comfort his mother but doing the opposite.

"Damn. How they let someone that come from them kind of genes in the Army?" Bonnie shook her head and went back into the house. Kevin stood there until the three of them disappeared then followed his mother inside.

Granny watched her grandkids go into what would be their new bedrooms; Peewee's at the back of the house and Candy's near Mae and Jabo's, close to the living room. All their toys and clothes had been moved in, just like they were at the old place. They were very excited, and Granny was too, and though she had her reservations, she kept them to herself. That Bonnie was sure giving them the evil eye when they got out of the car and didn't even say hello when Granny and the kids waved at her and Kevin. She didn't have a good feeling about that woman at all, but she hid her concern since the kids were so excited about their new life.

Candy came out of her room all smiles and saw Granny sitting on the couch. "When is Momma coming back?" she asked, crawling into Granny's lap. "Are you gonna stay with us?"

"Your momma and her new husband are coming back the day after tomorrow and until they do, I'll be here."

Peewee went out the back door to check out the yard to see if he would be able to play back there like he had at the other place. He was happy to see there were all kinds of things in the yard to discover. There was an old shed and a bench near it, which made his fantasy go wild with ideas on how to keep himself busy out there during what he was sure would be a ton of fights between Momma and her new husband. Peewee couldn't think of any reason why this time should be any different than the rest, even though he hoped it would be. Candy, in her ignorant bliss, took out her dolls while Granny went over to the kitchen to make supper.

* * *

Later that day, Bonnie went off to her weekly bingo game, then out to the bar for a couple drinks, and Kevin and his friend Eddie set out on their motorcycles. They were riding down the highway, weaving in and out of traffic and shouting at each other as if they were sitting next to each other in a limo. Both had thick-hipped chicks on the back and each of them thought they were the kings of the road. If you asked one of them separately, they would have said *they* were the leader of the pack and the other his best friend. It was true that Eddie McClendon was Kevin's best friend, but he was also Ruby McClendon's brother.

She was a girl who lived across the street from Kevin, and I'll get back to her a little later.

The four pulled over at Humboldt Park and decided to smoke a joint or two, or three.

"Man, what the hell you talkin' 'bout?" Kevin asked.

"I'm serious, bro. The police caught me in the back of my car!"

"Fellas, we're going for a bathroom walk," the girls announced.

"Cool, just don't forget who you drove here with." Kevin winked at the youngest girl with the largest hips. "Bitch," he said under his breath when the young lady was far enough away not to hear.

"Bro, pass me that joint." Eddie put his hand out, and Kevin gave him the joint. "You know Ruby's been askin' when you gonna come over and see that baby."

Kevin passed the spliff back after taking a big puff. "Speaking of bitches?" Kevin laughed at his own joke; Eddie didn't. "I'm just messing with you, man. Hell, I don't need to hear all this from you *and* from her. Especially not tonight when we tryin' ta get laid."

Eddie was referring to Renet, Ruby and Kevin's three-year-old baby girl. About four years before, Kevin had lied to Ruby about his age and the relationship quickly turned sexual. When Ruby got pregnant and told Kevin about it, he freaked out, saying, "Damn, girl, I can't have no kids. I'm only fourteen years old!" Since then, he'd seen the baby girl maybe once or twice, even though he and Eddie were best friends.

"Bro, you know I'm wit' you, but this is my sister, man," Eddie complained. "You ain't the only one sick of hearing about it."

"Look, man, let's just hit these chicks we got wit' us now and we can talk business later." Kevin was obviously uncomfortable with the whole thing that he would prefer to just forget.

"Business, nigga? This ain't no damn business, that's yo baby. If you ain't gonna send Ruby any damned money, you need to at least see the kid once in a while," Eddie argued, knowing that if he could get Kevin to go over there it would shut Ruby up, at least for a while.

"All right, man, hell, I'll go on over there tomorrow," Kevin promised. "But tonight, we gon' smash these chicks down!"

"That sounds like a plan," said Eddie.

Just then, the young ladies came walking back up. "You boys are going to have to take us somewhere to go to a bathroom, there was nothing open in this damn park."

Kevin looked over at Eddie, then said, "We can go to my house. My mom's out playing bingo or some shit." Kevin and Eddie laughed and high fived each other. The young ladies agreed and got back on the parked motorcycles. They left the park, speeding off into the last few moments of daylight.

Eddie couldn't help thinking about his sister, knowing how hard it had been for her these last few years. Even though Kevin was his friend, he knew eventually it would ruin their friendship because Kevin was a real deadbeat dad, and Eddie wasn't like that. He liked Kevin enough, but as time went on and he saw what kind of shit he pulled, he wasn't so sure how long the friendship would last.

When they got back to Kevin's and it was time to get the girls to have sex with them, Eddie decided he was too tired, and offered to take the one Kevin didn't want home.

For some weird reason, the younger girl stayed without her friend and thought it would be a good idea to have sex with Kevin. She regretted it when immediately afterwards, he told her to get her ass up if she wanted a ride home. It was two in the morning or thereabouts when Kevin, high on weed and driving recklessly through the streets of Buffalo's Eastside, finally made it back to Guilford Avenue. He saw his mom's car in the driveway and the light on, so he turned off the headlamp and parked his bike in the back, then snuck into Jabo's backyard, which wasn't hard to do since there was an open gate between the two properties.

For a few years now, this had been almost a nightly activity for Kevin, since he hid his stash in Jabo's shed. Unlike today, where you can get weed at dispensaries, back then it was highly illegal and some people, meaning a lot of black folks, went to jail for years even if they had just a little bit of grass on them. This was the reason Bonnie had a major problem with him smoking and possessing weed, and even though they were close, she told him she would call the police herself if that shit was anywhere near her or in the house. Kevin figured the shed was far enough away that if anyone got done for it, it wouldn't be him. Besides, no one ever went in the shed or even out to the backyard, for that matter, so he knew it would be safe.

Sitting on the old rusty bench, Kevin lit his joint and inhaled, gazing up at the moon. The warm night breeze made the experience even better. After about twenty minutes, he got up, hid the stash back into the wall of the old shed, and started down the driveway towards his house. He stopped abruptly, as if someone had called him by his first and last name, then glanced at the side door to Jabo's house and walked over to it, standing there for a moment. Then he took the key that was under the mat and slipped it into the lock. The door was unlocked, to his surprise, so he returned the key and silently entered the house.

Kevin eased the old wooden door shut behind him as to not wake up the sleeping family inside. He walked up the three steps into the kitchen and down the hall to the first bedroom that was now Peewee's. Kevin looked in on the sleeping boy and moved on to the next room, which was Jabo's. The door was open and the room empty. He passed by and looked inside the next room. This was Candy's.

He stood in the doorway staring at the sleeping child and noticed that the once-boring brown walls had been painted bright pink and the dresser and chest were lined with dolls. He heard a noise behind him and whipped around to see Granny standing in the hallway with a frying pan in her hand.

"What in the good name of God are you doing in this house, boy?"

Kevin started to shake. If there was one thing you did not do, it was mess with an old black lady with a frying pan in her hand. Kevin wanted to think of some clever answer fast, but he was so stoned he could only manage a lame excuse. "I wanted to see if Mae and Jabo were home yet."

"You know damn well they ain't home, so you better get your ass over to yours right this minute or I will hit you over the head with this pan so hard you'll fall into a coma. I'm gonna tell the police it was self-defense." She stood there waiting for him to go, which he did, right back out the way he came in. She shook her head in disbelief and locked the door behind him, then went back to the couch in the living room where she'd been sleeping.

chapter 8

Happy Fourth of July

"Girl, can you get the potato salad out of the refrigerator and put some foil on it? I forgot what I did with that top to the container," Oda-Lee said to Betty as she rushed around the kitchen.

"I got that stuff ready this morning, Momma," Betty said with a hint of sarcasm in her voice.

"Then tell me why the beans ain't done, since you got an answer to everything?"

"Lord, I hate when we rush for no reason. It's still early and we only going over to Jabo's for a cookout," Betty said with a six-in-the-morning attitude in her voice.

Betty and Oda-Lee always went back and forth like that but loved each other dearly.

"We won't be eating 'til midnight if I don't get over there and get this meat started on that grill, so come on." Oda-Lee went out the back door to put the last of the trays of meat in the car.

"Here we go...finally getting out of the house at the crack of dawn to start barbecuing. Great, just great." Betty followed Oda Lee out of the house.

* * *

Candy, Mae, and Peewee were in the backyard getting things ready for the cookout. Mae was taking the clothes off of the line while the kids picked up small bits of this and that. Kevin was mowing a small section of the yard that was covered with grass.

"Thank you, Kevin," Mae said. He abruptly turned off the raggedy lawn mower and started taking it back to the shed, pretending not to hear. "Thank you, Kevin," Mae said again, louder.

"Thanks for what?" He stopped what he was doing stared at her blankly.

"For mowing the lawn and helping out with the yard."

"Bitch, this is my granddaddy's house and that's the only reason I'm taking care of it. I don't know who you think you are, coming in here like you part of this family, bringing your crippled-ass daughter and your nappy-head-ass son here so my granddaddy can spend his hard-earned money on all of you. The only thanks that will ever be given here is when you all leave."

Mae was at a loss for words. She thought Kevin might be warming up to the idea of her and Jabo, but she couldn't have been more wrong. Kevin locked up the shed and sat on the bench with his arms folded, glaring at Mae, who stood there with her mouth open. The only thing that didn't stop her from bursting into tears was the bright and cheerful voice coming towards her.

"Good morning, everybody! Good morning!" Oda-Lee and Betty came rushing into the yard with boxes of seasoned meat, potato salad, and such. Kevin got up and went running over to them before Mae could get to her.

"Anie!"

"Come here, boy, and give yo Anie some shuga."

"Hi Candy, hi Peewee," Betty said in a low voice, still trying to wake up. The kids each gave their new relative a hug and continued to do what they were doing while Betty went to find herself a cup of coffee in the kitchen.

"Mae, did you get the grill all ready to be lit?" Oda-Lee asked. Mae tried to speak but still couldn't get a word out. "Mae, honey, what's wrong with you?"

"Nothing," Mae answered. "I was cutting some onions and I guess they're still messing with my eyes."

"What you mean onions? Hell, I'm the one prepared all this food, you ain't..." Oda-Lee then realized there was something besides onions going on, so she let it go. For now. "Oh, onions, right," she said with a sympathetic look. "Kevin, go get me some matches and some of that wood to put on this fire." As soon as he rounded the back of the shed, she pulled Mae to her and looked her in the eyes. "Look, girl, I want you to know that whatever it is, you can talk to me. You married my brother and I don't care who don't like it, you are my sister now and part of this family. Do you understand?" Mae nodded, fighting back tears. "Good. Now let's get this party started. And for God's sake, somebody go tell Bonnie to get her fat ass over here to help."

Kevin dropped a pile of wood next to the grill, along with a book of matches. "I'll do it, Anie."

* * *

By the afternoon, Marvin Gaye was softly playing on the portable radio and everybody was laughing and having a wonderful time. The ribs and chicken were about five minutes from being done, spirits were high, and stomachs were hungry. Right then, the drunken sounds of none other than Mr. Willie rang out in the driveway.

He is the first of three Willies you'll meet in this story. This one we call Mr. Willie.

Mr. Willie was an old flame of Anie's—one of those flames you wished had let turned to ash long ago. Not only the neighborhood drunk, he was always in the wrong place at the wrong time. He was hated by mostly everyone except the kids, who loved him because it was entertaining to watch him do dances and sing weird songs. Mr. Willie would not just sing a little bit of a song, no, he would sing the whole damn thing and do an entire dance, full out, from beginning to end, no matter what time of day, night, or location.

"Oh lord, here comes Mister Willie's drunk ass," Anie and Bonnie said in unison.

"Distant lover!" Mr. Willie screamed at the top of his lungs like he was on stage and leaned all the way back. Without missing one step, he entered the yard waving his arms over at Oda Lee. Betty started laughing.

"Oda-Lee, you better go over and get yo man," Jabo said.

"Willie, why don't you sit yo ass down somewhere," Anie said, completely embarrassed.

"Because I'm here to claim my queen!" He pulled an old shoe out of his pocket, better known at that time as a "Jelly." Jellies were cheap plastic shoes that mostly little girls and sometimes women wore. There were two sure things about Jellies, the price was cheap and they were guaranteed to fuck up your feet. Everybody tried to stop from laughing as Mr. Willie slid into the second verse of his sing. Mr. Willie was always drunk, so all the words sounded pretty much the same. He got to the climax of his routine and decided to end it with a couple of spins and kicks in the air while at the same time blowing fake kisses at Anie with his eyes closed—all in the name of love, you understand. Right in the middle of the second spin, he lost his balance and the Jelly went one way and he went the other, and that cheap-ass shoe landed on Mae's plate, right between the ribs and macaroni salad. His sorry ass was the second to land, right on top of the old grill, knocking it and all the barbecued meat right in the dirt.

Mortified, Anie started shoving potato salad in her mouth, trying to pretend the whole thing didn't happen.

"What in the hell is wrong with you? Get yo drunk ass up, Willie!" Jabo yelled.

"What the hell...is he okay?" Mae asked.

Kevin ran to help him out of the fire. "Mister Willie, are you okay?"

"I'm fine! But now I'm burning even more for my fiancée."

Everybody wanted to laugh, but they knew it wouldn't sit well with Anie, so they froze. That was when Bonnie and her four-hundred-pound ass let out a roar like a big bear, leaned back in her chair to grab a second wind to laugh again, and the back legs of the chair couldn't hold her anymore. The chair collapsed, shattering into a million pieces, like Goldie Hawn and Meryl Streep when they fell down in that final scene of *Death Becomes Her*. Somehow Bonnie ended upside down trying to get up, like a turtle on its back. Kevin tried his best to push her up, ripping her pants in the process, exposing the entire crack of her ass. That was the last straw. One by one, everyone laughed, some of them almost to the point of fainting.

"Now *this* is what I call a barbecue!" Jabo shouted.

Everyone in the yard laughed even more.

* * *

Once it got dark and the plates and food were cleared away, everyone lined up on the porch to watch the fireworks. With every bang and blast they got louder and louder. Mae stood next to Jabo, enjoying every minute.

"Ain't that pretty?" Oda-Lee said.

"Momma, look." Candy pointed at the colorful bursts of light filling the sky.

Bonnie and Betty looked at each other, both thinking about the entire incident earlier.

"Aw, cousin, you gotta admit that shit was funny," Betty said.

Bonnie laughed a bit but was definitely embarrassed.

"*Jabo!*" Mae screamed and everyone turned to see what the fuss was all about. She was holding Jabo as best she could as he slumped to the ground.

"Daddy!" Kevin yelled, and he and Bonnie started pushing everyone out of the way, especially Mae.

"Move yo ass out of the way, girl!" Bonnie said.

"Daddy, what's wrong? Are you okay?" Bonnie screamed over him. "Dial nine eleven, bitch, instead of standing there lookin' stupid," she said to Mae.

Mr. Willie, true to form, totally and inappropriately saying the wrong thing, said, "Who the hell says nine eleven?"

"Shut up, Mister Willie, this is serious!" Bonnie shrieked through her tears.

"Hell, I *am* serious, Miss Bonnie. I ain't never heard nobody in they right mind tell somebody to dial nine eleven."

Exasperated, Oda-Lee shoved Mr. Willie out of the way. "Back up, give the man some air."

Bonnie cradled Jabo in her arms until the ambulance arrived and whisked him away to Buffalo General Hospital.

chapter 5

Buffalo General Hospital

Everyone from the BBQ was now sitting in the emergency room, except for Mr. Willie, who was definitely not invited. Being the Fourth of July, the doctors were dealing with everything from dog bites to gunshot wounds. Kids were running around screaming, crying, and whining, and the place was a madhouse.

The family was quiet, worrying about Jabo, until Oda-Lee started singing the first few lines of "I Love the Lord, He Heard My Cry," and one by one, everyone joined in. This is a call and response song we all learned in church, one that the older deacons loved to sing. Of every negro spiritual, this was one you could clearly have imagined Harriet Tubman singing in the underground railroad. The song is so long and drawn out that by the time you get to the end, God will have either answered or you would have forgotten why you were asking him for help in the first place. Either way, you felt better and that was the point.

The song is so contagious that even some of the others in the waiting area began to sing along.

"What an amazing sound," a nurse said. You could tell by the look on her face that it was a far cry from the mass she attended, or whatever she was used to. The spirit was high and some of the folks who always wanted to sing or thought they had great voices started to throw in extra riffs and turns.

The head nurse, a very tall woman and over three hundred pounds with a name tag that read Bertha Mae Williams, came around the corner, hands on her hips. "Excuse me, but does this look like Buffalo General Baptist Church to y'all? This is a hospital and we need *quiet*."

Bonnie stopped singing. "We're sorry, ma'am, we didn't mean to—"

"Sorry didn't do it," Bertha Mae cut in. "Y'all did."

Anie stood up to face Big Bertha. "Girl, we heard you the first time, and if you don't get yo big bull-looking ass outta here, telling us we can't sang and pray in the hospital, where y'all got my brother back there doin' God knows what..." she shook her head. "Unless you comin' out here with an update, honey, we don't wanna hear it."

"Momma," Betty said gently, trying to calm Oda-Lee down, pulling her away from the huffing and puffing Bertha.

Bertha walked away with her head held high, mumbling under her breath, "Sang the damn song then, hell, they don't pay me enough to be in here fighting with y'all asses no way." She disappeared around the corner as quickly as she came.

Oda-Lee sat back down. "Don't Momma me. Hell, she come out here like she was the president's wife, loud-talking us while my brother is back there and ain't nobody giving me no updates." Anie's voice was trembling. She always stood for what was right, however, she was definitely dramatic. She'd just gone from getting ready to fight a bull to being a three-year-old girl whimpering because she didn't get what she wanted for Christmas.

"Oda-Lee, let's go get a soda pop, girl," Mae said. "I think we both need some fresh air."

"I think you right, child, I'm about to go to jail in here." They got up and headed down the hallway.

"Lord, I hope my husband is going to be okay. Oda-Lee, we only just got married!"

"He's gonna be fine, I'm sure of it. God ain't that cruel, and my brother is a tough old bastard. I've seen him go through worse. He just needs to take care of his sugar."

In black families, "sugar" was the word everybody used when talking about diabetes. I'm guessing it also worked against us because calling it sugar softened its impact, which was probably why people didn't take it as seriously as they should have.

"I know, Oda-Lee, I tell him all the time. He just does whatever the hell he wants to do."

"You need to put your foot down and stop letting him and everyone just walk over you, girl."

"I'm trying not to, but I don't wanna rock the boat. I already know they don't like me being with him," Mae said sadly.

"Sit down, girl, I wanna talk to you serious. Look, I don't give a damn if you married my brother for his money or for his damn kidney, he made his choice to be with you and that's that. I will never understand how people get so involved in other people's lives that they just hate who they with so much they keep trying to rip the folks apart. Hell, Jabo is a grown-ass man and if he wanted to marry a *man*, I'd be fine with it. I'd make fun of his punk ass, but I'd be fine with it. You need to get you a backbone and stop letting everyone push you in all directions. Listen, Mae, life brings you ups and downs, and none of us would know the good if it weren't for the bad. Same goes for people, right? Life brings you good folks and it brings you bad folks. At the end of the day, you just gotta be glad that God continues to bring you life at all. Tomorrow isn't promised to any one of us, but if you are blessed to see it, why the hell would you allow bad people and bad situations make you have a bad damn day? That's just stupid to me. Every day you are able to open your eyes is a good day and another chance for you to get it right."

"Thank you, Oda-Lee. You always know the right thing to say...and when to say it."

"Mae, it's not knowing what to say, it's knowing what *not* to say and to just act. There are no mistakes, remember that, only choices we make, and when we make them, we need to stand by them. Execute them and see them through, don't let them execute us. We always stop when things don't go in our favor and call it failure instead of keeping on until it works! I know what I'm talkin' 'bout, now. I watched my daddy lose everything, but he kept on planting and watering the fields that hadn't produced nothin' for two solid years. That third year we had the perfect rainfall and the ground was nourished to perfection. He ended up with the best crop he had ever had and was able to sell it all and get everything back he'd lost and then some. We made enough to live on for five years. Mae, just think of what would have happened if he'd chucked it all in and gave up the day he lost everything. Girl, let the bill collectors call, let the people send notices in your mailbox, but do not give up hope that things will change for the better."

"That's so true, Oda-Lee. I didn't give up hope and look who I married," Mae said with a sad smile. "He has to make it. He has to!"

"He will, but you missing the point. Look in the mirror and say to yourself, 'Look at who *he* married!' You're somebody too, which is even more of a reason to let people talk all they want while you stand your ground and speak your mind, even if it's only through your actions. Mae, it's between you and Jabo and that's all there is to it."

"Oda-Lee, you are just the best. You remind me of my momma." Mae embraced her sister-in-law.

"Now hold on, I ain't *that* damn old." They both laughed. Oda-Lee caught the time from a clock up on a wall. "We been talking for forty-five minutes and we still ain't found no damn pop! Do you even know where the machine is?"

"No, I thought you did."

"Girl, I am telling you, when I turn this corner there better be a sign that says Pepsi or you in trouble." They walked to the end of the hall and turned but there was no sign, only another long corridor. "Mae, what the hell!?" Oda-Lee laughed.

"Remember, Oda-Lee, there will be good days and bad days but in the end, there are only choices. This will work out, don't worry," Mae said to Oda-lee with a smile.

"Yeah, for your sake you better hope I'm right!"

They walked down the hall, hoping they'd be lucky around the next corner.

* * *

In the waiting room everyone was getting restless, but finally Mae and Oda-Lee turned up with cans of Pepsi for everyone. Mae tried to hand one to Bonnie, but she shook her head and kept her arms folded, so Mae gave the pop to Betty instead.

"Thank you, Auntie Mae," Betty said with a cheeky smile.

Dr. Wright stepped into the room. "Hello, everyone, I have an update on Mister Burder. I'll need the next of kin to come with me."

Bonnie jumped up. "I'm his daughter, I'm over all of his business and I was made his estate guard within the last five years."

"Sit yo ass down," Oda-Lee said loudly. "Mae is his wife. What the hell is an estate guard anyway? What damn estate? Two old-ass houses on Guilford Avenue? Girl, sit yo ass down, Dr. Wright didn't say he was dead."

"I know that, but I'm the one that if anything should happen Daddy said I was—"

"I don't care what you said he said...." Oda-Lee was getting louder, and Dr. Wright was about to put an end to it when Mae spoke up.

"I'm his wife now, so shut the hell up, Bonnie!" Mae screamed at the top of her voice. The room went quiet. She even startled Dr. Wright. "Dr. Wright, we don't have time for all of this, so I'm coming with you."

"It's fine for you both to come," Dr. Wright said to Bonnie and Mae.

"I'm coming too. Hell, Mae, you just learned how to fight, so you gon' need backup. Besides, y'all gon' need a referee." Oda-Lee snatched up her purse.

The three of them followed the doctor into the next room. "Sit down, please. I know you all are aware Mister Burder has been suffering from diabetes for the last two years."

"Yes, Doctor, but he told me it was under control," Mae said.

"It is. But what we *didn't* know is that he has stage three cancer and cirrhosis of the liver." Dr. Wright let that sink in for a moment.

"Lord Jesus," Oda whispered, covering her mouth.

"We are running some tests to see how progressed his condition is, but Mister Burder also has a sore on his left leg that hasn't healed in quite some time. It somehow got infected, so there is a chance we may have to amputate the leg."

Mae looked confused. "A sore on his leg? He never mentioned nothing to me about a sore and I sure haven't seen it."

"What the hell, Mae?" screamed Bonnie. "You lay yo ass up there with my daddy every night and you didn't know he had a sore on his leg? I swear I knew you'd be too concerned about his money to inspect the man who you sleep with every night."

"No, I didn't because his dick works fine! Did *you* know he had that on his leg, Bonnie? You his daughter."

"Not to mention his damned estate guard," Oda-Lee cracked.

Dr. Wright raised her hand. "Please, ladies, it's not something anyone would or could have noticed. In fact, it took Mister Burder himself some time to realize it was there. It was a wound that had healed over, but an infection spread internally. On the outside, it looks more like a bump than anything else. It's not the first time I've seen an injury like this. Missus Burder, please go out there and tell your family that he is stable and we're keeping him here for a while. They can all go home, get some rest, and we'll funnel the information and updates through you."

The three women went back into the waiting area, their faces long.

"Come on, Kevin," said Bonnie, "we gonna go and get some things straight."

Mae sat down next to Peewee and Candy. "Peewee, go with Betty and take your sister home, then put her to bed. Oda-Lee and I are going to stay here at the hospital for a while."

"Okay, Momma. Is everything gonna be all right?"

"It's gonna be fine," she said, glancing up at Oda-Lee, who was looking at her with the same concerned face.

They all started to walk out the door, then Candy turned around. "I wanna stay with you, Momma."

"Girl, you go with your brother and Betty. I gotta stay here at the hospital." Tears started to roll down Candy's cheeks. "Stop that crying before I give you something to cry about."

"Mae, don't be so mean to that poor child. Take it out on Bonnie instead!" Oda-Lee went over to Candy and stroked her head. "You go on, child, yo Momma'll be home soon."

Oda-Lee sat back down. "It's going to be a long road, Mae," she said. "I hope you ready for it."

"Yes, Oda-Lee, tonight's gonna be crazy."

"Child, I don't mean tonight. I mean whatever comes out of this thing with Jabo. That girl is gonna drive you to hell, so you better get yourself ready." She was talking about Bonnie.

* * *

Betty dropped Peewee and Candy off at the house and went home.

"Why did we leave Momma there, Peewee?" Candy asked as he tucked her into her bed.

"'Cause Jabo's not feeling well, and Momma needs to make sure he'll be sleeping all right." Peewee gave Candy her night medication.

"Is he going to die, Peewee?" she asked.

"No, Candy, he's gonna be okay. You go to sleep, all right? Momma will be home soon. I love you, Candy."

"I love you too." Candy fell asleep almost immediately.

Peewee sat there looking at her for the longest time, realizing how beautiful and innocent she was, really noticing beauty in her face he hadn't taken the time to see before. He smiled and stroked her hair. It had been a very long day.

Peewee finally got up and went into his room, put on his Walkman headphones, and lit up a joint he had stashed away. Even though he was almost sixteen and thought he was the man, in reality he was just a lightweight, and before long he got drowsy and dozed off.

chapter 10

The Morning After

Mae didn't get in until around five in the morning. She didn't want to leave Jabo alone after Dr. Wright had given him the news, and while waiting for him to finally fall asleep, she did too.

Bright and early the next day, Candy woke up and called out to Peewee, "Is Momma home yet?"

He came into her room sleepily, rubbing his eyes. "Yeah, I think I heard her come in. Man, I slept so good last night. I bet Momma's tired. How about we surprise her and give you a bath so she don't have to?"

Candy's eyes lit up. She didn't particularly care for her daily baths, but she had to take them because of the weird smell, as well as making sure she didn't get bed sores or diaper rash.

Peewee let water into the bath then went and got Candy to help her into the tub. He stood at the toilet to take a piss.

"Hey, Peepee," giggled Candy. "Peepee, Peepee...."

Peewee didn't mind her calling him that. He didn't mind much of anything she did. He loved his little sister and felt very protective of her. When he was done, he went over to the tub and gave her a kiss

54

on the cheek. "Here is the towel coming in for a landing," he teased, coming in closer to her as if he was landing a 747 on her shoulders. Candy kept giggling as he scrubbed her all over. Then he started to wash her leg, and Candy let out a yelp. "What's wrong?" Peewee asked, looking at her with concern.

"My leg hurts."

"Where?" he asked, and just as he was about to take a closer look, the door came flying open. Peewee was so shocked he jumped and dropped the rag on the floor.

"Boy, get yo ass outta here, you're just making a mess. Look, you got water all over the floor," Mae said.

Peewee ran out of the bathroom and went back into his room, got dressed, then ran out the back door to go into the yard. He stopped at the mat in front of the door. Mae came to the back steps and could see Peewee shaking and moving the mat around.

"Where is the damn key?" Peewee said under his breath.

"What key?" Mae yelled down to a startled Peewee who didn't know she was standing there.

"Momma!" Candy called from the bathroom.

Mae grimaced. "Oh my God, y'all kids about to drive me up a wall. I'm comin', Candy!"

Peewee dropped the mat and ran off to see what other kind of trouble he could get into without anyone seeing him.

chapter 11

A Visitor

"There he is," Oda-Lee said when the tall, handsome man walked out of the Greyhound Bus station. "Charles! Over here!"

"Anie, look at you. How the hell are you?"

"Look at me? Look at *you*. You done grown up!" They both started laughing. Charles was Oda-Lee and Jabo's nephew. His father had been estranged from the family and then died some years back, but they'd always kept in touch with Charles. At one point, he decided he wanted to make a new life for himself up north and work in the steel mills like everybody else, so Jabo agreed to refer him. He was pretty certain he could get a capable young man like Charles a job and even assured him there would be a job waiting on him when he finally made the move to Buffalo.

"Well, here I am," Charles announced.

"Yeah, you sure are, and we are so glad to have you," Oda-Lee said warmly.

They got in the car and drove off from the bus station.

"So how's everybody doing?"

"Bonnie is fine, about to marry some Puerto Rican man named Benny and bring him and his three kids over here to live with her. Child, I do not know how that's gonna work out." Charles just kept nodding his head as Oda-Lee continued giving her family report. "And Betty, she's still just being Betty. Sometime she up, sometime she down, tough keeping that girl in the middle. Anyway, she's dating this guy named Willie and I think he gon' ask her to marry him. But you know you can never tell with these boys these days." They exchanged a knowing smile. "Kevin going into the Army in a month, and Jabo got married to a nice woman named Mae."

"Wait, Jabo got married? Well, I'll be damned. Never thought I'd hear that!"

"Yeah, she got three kids, Candy, Peewee, and Gerry, but the oldest, he been off in the Army this whole time, so I never met him."

"What's she like, this Mae?" Charles wanted to know, still not being able to believe his Uncle Jabo had tied the knot with someone.

"Well, Mae used to be known as the town ho, but she come a long way, and everybody deserves a chance to make it better, Jesus knows. She is just as pretty as she can be but hasn't had it good. Bonnie can't stand her and is always giving her a hard time. But you know me, I love everybody, child. I ain't got time to be worried about other folks' shit no way."

"That's what I love about you, Anie." Charles flashed her his biggest, white-teethed smile. "I heard from my momma that Jabo lost a leg, is that right?"

"Oh, it's been hard on everybody, but he's coming along now. We all pitching in to help but he ain't the only one in the house with one leg." Oda-Lee kind of chuckled to herself, realizing that she didn't mean to make it sound comical. Charles looked over at her, totally confused. "You'll see what I mean when we get to the house," she said.

"Okay. So is Jabo officially retired now?"

"Yeah, baby, he can't do nothing but sit around and hope to get better. He also got the cancer too, but they say it's progressing slowly.

He'll be glad to see you, that's for sure. Let me get you on over to that house so everybody can see what a fine young man you've become."

* * *

"Anyone home?" Oda-Lee shouted when she and Charles entered the house.

"We're in the living room, come on in," Jabo called from his wheelchair.

"Look what the cat drug in from the bus station."

Charles came around the corner and Jabo just about fell off his chair. "Boy, you all grown up," he said in surprise. "Finally grew into them lips. Charles, this is my wife Mae."

"Hello, Mae, nice to meet you," Charles said.

"Nice to meet you too, Charles."

"Better not be *too* nice," Oda-Lee said under her breath.

"Daddy! Where you at?"

Jabo grimaced. "That's yo cousin Bonnie coming in with her loud ass."

"Hey there, Charlie," Bonnie said in her booming voice.

"You lookin' good, Bonnie." Charles gave her a hug, though he was having a hard time getting his arms around her.

"Hell, you must need glasses, boy, she looks like a ox," Jabo said and cracked up laughing. "I keep on her about her weight, but all she does is close her ears and open her mouth!"

"Daddy, you better stop talking that shit about me."

"Charlie, would you like me to take your things?" Mae asked. "Are you hungry?"

"He's not, but you are!" Bonnie said.

"Y'all a mess if I ever seen one." Oda-Lee rolled her eyes up to the heavens.

Charles did his best to ignore the family feud he'd just found out about, wondering what the hell he'd gotten himself into. "Yes, Mae, I wouldn't mind having something to eat."

She headed into the kitchen. "Well, come on then, lemme fix you a plate."

"So, boy, I'm glad to have you here. I got you all set up. Thirty-two years as a supervisor at Bethlehem Steel still counts for something, so I got you a nice job with plenty of room to advance if you good."

"Thank you, Jabo. I certainly do appreciate it," said Charles.

"But if you get there and act a fool in my company, not only are you gonna lose your job, I'mma kick yo ass. You hear me, boy?"

Charles smirked. "Yes, Jabo, I hear you."

"All right, then, get on in there and get yo'self something to eat. You can stay here till you get yo'self going out here, which better be within the next month or so."

"Thanks, Jabo, I really do appreciate what ya doing for me," said the tall, good-looking young man.

Charles walked into the kitchen. Oda-Lee watched him over the top of her glasses, her head tilted down. She sat back slowly in her chair shaking her head with a look on her face that said it all. She knew one way or another this was about to be a big, fat, ugly mess.

chapter 12

Sunday Morning

Sundays were church days in Oda-Lee's house.

"I know you ain't just layin' around thinking you ain't going to go to church, are you, Betty?" Oda-Lee yelled into her room while Betty looked like she was still asleep.

"Betty, girl, you know I'm not going to be running around here waiting on you to iron my dress. I asked you nicely last night to do it for me and you promised you would. Now you still in bed and the dress look like somebody slept on it."

"Momma, I'm getting up now. We don't even have to be there until—"

"Never mind when we have to be there. I like to be ready when I like to be ready. Aw, hell, girl, just forget it." Oda-Lee shook her head as she always did when something didn't go her way.

A few minutes later she magically appeared in Betty's doorway wearing another dress, all ready to go. "I'm going to Sunday School and Reverend Bowman likes to get started early. They need me to take the minutes, open up the church, and help get things going. Then I need to get the chicken ready for the dinners that we sellin' to the visiting church for this afternoon. I got a lot to do and I don't need you slow-as-sin' around. You know we ain't got but eight members, so I gotta do a thousand jobs." Oda-Lee started down the stairs and Betty followed. "And if you ain't coming to church, I want this house cleaned up when I get back. You should be ashamed of yo'self, Betty, not going to church. God don't like ugly, and he ain't too crazy about pretty."

"Momma, you told me last night we'd be leaving the house at nine and now you're..." Betty couldn't finish her sentence because Oda-Lee walked out of the house and slammed the door in her face.

Betty went over to the window and watched Oda-Lee lock the front door then head towards the steps, still fussing. "I know you don't think I'm gonna to let you just sit up on Sunday in my house all damn day and not go to church. No! No!"

"Ugh, Momma, please," Betty groaned. "Lord, she get on my damn nerves, I hope she falls flat on her ass!" Just as Betty said it, Oda-Lee's heel got caught in a crack in the step.

"Lord help me Jesus!" *Boom!* "Father God!" *Boom!* "Heavenly host!" *Boom!* "Have mercy on me, Lord!" she shrieked as she bounced down all ten wooden stairs. Her purse went flying in the opposite direction of her knees, her stockings ripped, her glasses flew, and she fell all the way down to the last stair, right into the grass and indeed on her ass. When she started rolling and trying to get up, she stepped right into a pile of fresh dog shit. "Jesus, no Lord! Betty! Betty!"

"Oh my God!" Betty cried. "I didn't mean it!" She ran outside to help a sobbing Oda-Lee off the grass.

"Lord, Jesus, get my purse, Betty. Heavens, why this morning, Lord? And why *me*? This ain't nothin' but the devil tryin' to keep me from God!" Thanks to an excess of padding on Oda-Lee's rear, she was not hurt.

* * *

Oda-Lee wasn't the only person the devil was visiting that morning. He went right over to Mae and Jabo's house as soon as he'd finished with Oda-Lee. This was the first Sunday Jabo would be going to church since his operation, and tensions were running high, especially with a guest in the house whose bedroom was the living room since all the spare rooms had long been taken. Jabo hoped Charles would find a place soon, but it didn't look like it would be today.

Charles was in the kitchen making breakfast. Mae went in to take care of Candy. Peewee had gone fishing with his father Willie (yes, another Willie), and they always left at the crack of dawn. Jabo wasn't all that big on going to church himself, but with his illness and all the things he was facing, he decided he better start going. Everybody always wants the holy ghost when they think they going to see the King soon.

Mae went into Candy's room to wake her up and saw that she was sitting on the edge of the bed crying. "What's wrong, Candy? You okay?"

Candy shook her head because she knew that whatever it was, she was gonna be in trouble.

"Candy? There's got to be something wrong or you wouldn't be cryin'," Mae said, her voice raised enough to make Candy even more scared. Candy pointed down and moved over a bit and all Mae could see was blood. She hugged her, then smiled at her before moving her aside. "Oh, girl, that's okay, you gonna be all right." But she wasn't too sure, surprising as it was that at this age and with her condition Candy had started her period. She took the sheets off the bed and put them in the closet to be washed and went back to getting Jabo ready.

chapter 13

Bingo

Kevin was pissed, pacing back and forth in the yard behind the shed.

"Who the fuck been in my shit?" he ranted.

Whereas nowadays you can hit any corner in California and complain of "glaucoma" and you can come in and leave with whatever you want, at that time, weed was a bit harder to come by. Hell, they even got different flavors now. Back then there were no dispensaries, and Kevin had spent all the money Jabo had given him on that stash. He did have an idea who was pinching it but couldn't say anything because hell, who was he gonna tell? They'd both be in just as much trouble. "They won't get no more, though, I know that." He stuffed what little was left in the bag in his pocket and headed back into the house.

Tonight was bingo, which meant Bonnie would be out most of the evening and Kevin would have the house to himself. She was in the kitchen talking to someone on the phone when Kevin entered, shutting the door a little too hard, pissed about his shit being stolen.

Bonnie pulled the phone away from her ear. "Boy, stop slamming my damn door!" she said when he started rummaging through the cupboards for a bag of potato chips or something to kill the munchies. "Why the hell do you wear so much of that stinkin'-ass Brut cologne?" (To hide the smell of weed, of course.)

Kevin ignored her and left the kitchen, not finding what he wanted.

"Anyway, girl, let me tell you, this bitch drives my daddy's car, uses his credit cards, and makes herself right at home while my momma sitting over there in her house and can't hardly pay the bills. Not only that, but you *know* my momma is way better looking than that ugly-ass Mae. Anie is always telling me to be nice to her and that I should be ashamed of myself, but now she's done gone and decided to—" Bonnie stopped dead in her tracks, because the person on the other end said something that almost made her as mad at them as she was about the situation. "What? Girl, I'll kick yo ass and die before I call that woman Momma."

Kevin poked his head around the corner of the kitchen. "Momma, you cooking before you go to bingo tonight or what?"

"Naw, I ain't going to bingo tonight. Girl, I gotta fix this boy something to eat before he makes me lose my mind. I'll talk to you later." Bonnie hung up the phone and Kevin came and sat down across from her at the table.

"Look at you, still a momma's boy. What you gonna do in a month when you in the Army?"

"Well, somebody is cooking three meals a day at the same time every day," Kevin said sarcastically.

"Smart ass." Bonnie looked at him out of the corner of her eye and smiled.

"Why aren't you going to bingo?"

"Because that bitch next door decided she needed to ruin my life even more by coming to *my* bingo night."

"Momma, you can't just give up your shit because of her! Go to another one, they have more than one in the city. Look, you gon' be okay here all by yourself when I'm gone?" Kevin asked carefully.

Bonnie burst into tears. "Lord, I don't want you to go out there, boy. You gon' get killed. How the hell the Army gon' make a man outta you if they sending you back in a damn box?"

Kevin had never seen his mother like that before. In all his years, he'd seen Bonnie cry maybe once, and that was when she was watching some wack-ass soap opera.

"Don't you worry, I'll be fine, I swear. I just don't want you to be sitting here all alone worrying about me. I know you don't go over to Daddy's much anymore, so I don't want you here by yourself," Kevin said, and he meant it—for the most part. What he really needed was his mother missing him so much she sent him non-stop care packages and letters.

Bonnie snapped right out of her tears. "Hell naw I ain't going over with that bitch living there, using my father and taking all his money, freeloadin' and making a fool outta him and the rest of us."

Kevin had heard this so many times he was sick of the names Mae, Candy, and Peewee, and would have been happy for them to be out of their lives, but he couldn't do anything about that. Not right now, anyway.

"We were talking about *you*," Kevin said, bringing her back on track. "You go on to bingo tonight and show that bitch who's boss."

Bonnie started whimpering again. "Okay, yeah, you right. I'll be okay, don't worry, I got my friends." The phone rang and Bonnie answered it, sniffing and puffing. "Hello?" she said with the dry, cracked voice of sadness. "Yeah, I'm going to bingo. I'll come over and get you." She hung the phone up grinned at Kevin, mainly because he'd convinced her to go.

* * *

Charles was out having dinner with some friends, Peewee was in his room lost in his headphones, and Mae was fixing to go to Friday night bingo, which was a new thing for her since Jabo had lost his leg. At some point she decided to start doing other things to get her out of the house once in a while, or else she'd go crazy.

"Girl, stop splashin' that water all around, you're getting it all over the floor," Mae scolded as she helped Candy out of the tub. Preoccupied by the thoughts of bingo and other things, she dried Candy off, slipped her into her pajamas, and tucked her into bed. "You lay here and close your eyes and go to sleep. I'll come and check in on you before I leave."

"Okay, Momma." Candy laid back into her bed with her doll clutched in her arms.

Mae went into the dining area to get her things out of the cabinet.

"Where the hell you going tonight, Mae?" Jabo said with more concern than anger. "That girl needs you to be around sometimes," he said, glaring at her over the top of his glasses and looking exactly like Oda-Lee.

"I'm here almost every night, Jabo, damn! I'm just going to bingo." Mae smacked her lips and rolled her eyes, making sure he didn't see how frustrated she was, wishing he would just go and watch TV like he always did.

"Okay, well, I'll be sure to check in on her. She's just a baby and needs more attention than we all been givin' her, that's all."

"She loves it when you look in on her, Jabo, so you do that. Oh my goodness, it's almost six forty-five, I'm gonna be late." Mae took her bingo stick and all her supplies and ran out the front door.

"Lord, what am I gonna do with that damned woman?" He wheeled his chair over to the kitchen area and opened the refrigerator door, gazing in. He thought he heard music coming from the basement, which was now Charles's makeshift room, as well as someone singing next door. "I'mma eat some of these pork rinds, check in on that baby, then take my ass to bed and watch some TV." He crunched his way out of the kitchen and into the bedroom.

A while later, the house was near quiet, even though it was only about nine, and the only thing that could be heard were the faint sounds of the show *Gunsmoke* coming from the TV in the master bedroom.

In Candy's room, the silhouette of a man appeared in the doorway, then entered the room and went over to the edge of the bed. He leaned in to kiss her forehead. His lips lingered longer than appropriate for the kind of kiss you should give a child. He moved from her forehead down to her lips and stuck his tongue in between them. Candy shifted her body slightly, but the man was not worried. With all of the medication she took, Candy would sleep through an earthquake.

He undid his belt and took off his pants, letting them fall to the floor, climbed into the small bed, and lay down behind her. He stopped for a moment and listened for any sounds other than the TV, and when he was sure no one was coming, he began to move his hands down her body. Then he removed her underpants and held onto her small body. Breathing heavily, he pushed his pelvis forward, and he began doing the unthinkable. When he was finished, he quickly got up, put his pants back on, and left Candy's room.

The next morning, Mae was in the kitchen cooking breakfast for the family. You could smell the bacon all the way to the corner. She was talking to one of her sisters on the phone when Candy came crawling into the kitchen.

"Momma," Candy said.

"Hold on, girl, you see I'm on the phone, don't you?" Mae continued her conversation while Candy sat in the kitchen waiting for her to get off the phone. When Mae hung up the phone, the side door to the kitchen opened and Bonnie barged into the house.

"Is Daddy around?" she asked dryly.

"Yes, Charles took him to the drug store to get his medication and get him out of the house, so he should be back soon," Mae said.

"That means he ain't around, then." Bonnie rolled her eyes and walked out of the house.

"Bonnie!" Mae called after her. "Bonnie?!" The door slammed behind her. Mae stood in the kitchen staring at the door, unable to believe someone could be so damn stupid, until the smoke detector started screaming.

"Momma!" Candy screamed as a cloud of smoke started rising out of the skillet.

Mae turned and saw the smoke rising up. "Get out of the way girl," she said, almost tripping over Candy running to fan the smoke detector. "Girl, I said get out of my damn way!" Candy crawled out of the kitchen.

Mae took the skillet and threw it into the sink, bacon and all, and began to cry. "I hate this damn house," Mae said, then sat in the middle of the kitchen, her face in her hands, trying to hide her tears. In the midst of her tantrum, she noticed a small figure in the kitchen doorway. Candy sat there with tears in her eyes.

Mae reached her arms out to Candy, who crawled over to her and fell into her mother's arms. This was probably the first sign of affection Mae had shown Candy in a long time, and to Candy it meant the world. The two of them held each other until Mae looked at her and they both started smiling and then laughing.

"Come on, girl, we both need to go outside for some fresh air." Mae helped Candy up.

"I love you, Momma," said Candy.

"Me too," Mae said.

chapter 14

The Overstayed Welcome

"Dinner is served," Mae said after setting platters of neckbones, macaroni and cheese, potato salad, candied yams, and sweet tea to top it all off on the table.

"This looks so good," Charles said.

"Thank you, Charles, but it was nothing, really." Mae smiled and handed him the spoon for the yams.

"I always did like good cookin'. My momma can't cook at all." They laughed.

"Hurry up in there, dis ain't no conference 'bout the food." Jabo wheeled himself to the table, not nearly the confident, striking man he was in the months before his amputation and recovery.

His illness had taken its toll, and the cancer wasn't getting much better either. He'd lost weight and had become less patient. Not only that, but Charles was still around. Dinnertime was the time Jabo hated the most, and he was determined to get Charles out of there ASAP so he could enjoy his last days in peace and quiet with his wife and family.

"Jabo, I'm coming as soon as I can. Hell, you just yell and yell and forget how long I've been in here slaving over this!" Mae yelled out from the kitchen.

Peewee looked at Jabo, then towards the kitchen where Mae and Charles were. He had never actually heard his momma speak harshly like that. Well, except to him and Candy, though never to Jabo.

"Girl, don't make me get up outta this damn chair."

"Get on up if you want to. Go ahead," said Mae, and she and Charles laughed quietly to themselves.

"Momma, I don't want none of the yellow stuff," Candy said, frowning and pointing to the yams.

"Girl, shut yo ass up and eat them yams. And anyway, they orange."

When Mae had come out of the kitchen, Jabo couldn't believe his eyes. "Where the hell you think you going all dressed up like that?" he asked, looking at her in a nice new black skirt and a yellow and black sleeveless blouse, heels, and makeup. "You look like a two-dollar ho. Take that shit off. You ain't never wore that shit before, so don't start wearing it now."

Charles took a bite of his food then tried to change the subject with a full mouth, but it completely backfired. "This sure is good, Mae."

Jabo slammed his spoon down on the table. "Good? What the hell you saying *good* to, like you a dog just getting some damn food for the first time?"

Charles forgot that his uncle Jabo used to be the most easy-going man alive, and if it had been any other day and any other time, he might not have reacted the way he did. In truth, there was one thing Jabo hated to hear at the dinner table, and that was when someone said that the food was *good*. He had never acted this way before, but there was a lot more going on inside Jabo's heart and mind than anyone knew, and they were about to find out.

"Jabo, I'm sorry I—"

"Sorry my ass. Sorry didn't do it, you did!" (Damn man stole that line from Bertha the nurse!) "And another thing," Jabo shouted when Charles tried to start eating again, "you need to get yo ass outta my goddamn house and find yo own place to live. I said you could stay here a month and it's been way longer than that. I know you making money, so I want you out tomorrow. No, as a matter fact, tonight."

"Calm down, Jabo, that don't make no sense for you to be so damn mean to Charles," Mae said.

Jabo stared at Mae. "Who the hell are you defending in my house, Mae? If you gonna defend anyone, it better be me!"

Candy started crying as they all yelled at each other.

"Girl, you shut up," Mae snapped.

"Bitch, don't tell her to shut up. You don't do anything but treat that child like she a burden. Look at her, all you do is feed her. She's just gettin' fatter and fatter! You ain't concerned with nothing but yourself. You don't do nothing with her, no exercise, nothing!" Jabo shouted. "Now I know how it is to have only one leg and feel like don't nobody give a rat's nuts about how I'm really doing." He stormed away in his chair and didn't notice that it got stuck on the tablecloth, and he ended up pulling everything down on the floor.

Mae jumped up. "Jabo! What the hell is wrong with you!" she screamed, still trying to look cute as the food crashed to the floor.

"I bought all this food, bitch, and I'll do whatever I want with it." Jabo angrily rolled off to the back of the house.

Mae got up and ran into the kitchen and Charles ambled after her, leaving Peewee and Candy alone at the table.

"Peewee," Candy said in a small voice, "I gotta go to the bathroom."

"Come on, I'll help you." He helped his sister out of her chair, leaving the carnage of the dining table.

Knowing his mother's pattern, Peewee thought, *Now is the beginning of the end....*

Time to Say Goodbye

Tomorrow was the day Kevin would go off to boot camp, and it couldn't have come soon enough for Mae. One down, the rest to go. Tensions with just about every one of Jabo's family members were high, except for Oda-Lee, who stood by Mae come hell or high water. At least she thought so. But the next months would prove a test of that bond.

The night before Kevin was to leave, there was a farewell dinner at the house and Jabo was more grouchy than ever. He sat in front of the TV, and Candy was usually somewhere on the floor around his feet with her dolls, as happy as could be. Who the hell knew where Peewee was, he just came in when he felt like it or smelled food. Charles had been out of the house for a while so that wasn't an issue anymore...for now.

Because Kevin had to get up early and Jabo and Oda-Lee were set to see him off with Bonnie, dinner didn't last long, and everyone went home early. Mae was glad about that, there being no arguments for a change. About to go out of her mind with everything going on, Candy worried her especially, with all the weight she was gaining and looking so bloated. She tried to put the thought out of her mind that her medical life expectancy was only fifteen. Actually, Candy always seemed to feel fine, but now she was just eating and sleeping, so Mae decided she would take Candy to the doctor the first opportunity she had. For now, it was time to go to sleep, and after Mae had given Candy her bath and put her to bed, she left Jabo snoring in front of the TV in the living room. She did the dishes and a few things around the house, and heard Peewee come in and go into his room. When all was said and done, she finally got into bed around one in the morning.

As soon as the house fell into silence, the familiar figure came out from the shadows and made his way towards Candy's bedroom, being careful not to make any noises until he got into her room and shut the door. By now, he knew nothing could wake up anyone in the house. As soon as he got into Candy's room and shut the door, he pulled his pants down to his knees and began to play with himself while he watched the baby girl lying there in her diapers and baby-doll jammies.

He would've liked to prolong the act, but he wasn't about to risk getting caught, so he pulled her up into a sitting position and shoved his penis into her mouth, prying the sleeping girl's lips apart.

"Suck on it," he whispered harshly to the half-asleep child as he held the back of her head and forced the thing in her mouth until she started to gag. "Fuck this," he said, then laid her down onto the bed and took off her diaper. Candy was still fast asleep and, luckily for her, didn't even know she was in the world when he got on top of her little body and started to rape her...hard. He didn't give a thought to the fact that he might be ripping her apart. He just pushed and pulled until he came.

After he finished, he rolled off her like she was nothing and pulled on his pants. He looked at Candy for another long minute, then left the room without even putting another diaper on her. He just went back the way he came, closing the door behind him.

* * *

"My boy, the day has finally come," Oda-Lee said with a tear in her eye. "Anie loves you, and I don't want you to ever forget that. Make sure you be safe out there." She embraced Kevin and squeezed him tight.

"Boy, you know what I taught you? Now is the time for you to start being the man I always knew you could be," said Jabo, trying not to show too much emotion.

"June Bug," Betty said to her cousin, the name she had so often called him, "you know I love you, cousin, so keep in touch and we'll see each other soon." Betty gave Kevin a high-five.

"I love you all, you know that," he said sweetly. "I will be fine, so please don't worry yo asses about me. You all need to take care of Bonnie, all right? She gonna need you." Kevin kissed them all on their cheeks and waved goodbye as he boarded the Greyhound bus. He looked out the window, still waving goodbye but happy to finally be out of the house and from under his mother's thumb.

As they headed back to the car, Jabo said, "I'm gonna miss that boy."

"Yes, well, he is in God's hands now," said Oda-Lee.

"God's hands? Hell, you act like he dead or something, Oda-Lee. Shit."

"Jabo, don't you start in with me. You know exactly what I mean." These two were brother and sister for sure, because no matter how old they got, they were always fighting. Jabo could tease and laugh and shoot the shit about Oda-Lee, but no one else better!

"Can you wait a second, Oda-Lee? You just ramming me in the car like a wild animal or something," he said as she "helped" him into the passenger side of the car while Betty folded up the wheelchair and put it in the trunk. Oda-Lee closed the door and got into the driver's seat. "Oh Lord, now Jesus, if you ever heard any of my prayers, please hear this one and get us home safe," Jabo said with a smirk, shaking his head. "You know what, you are getting closer to being more of a bastard every day, brother," Oda-Lee said. "What is your problem? You've been really snappy with everybody lately. 'Cause lemme say, I'm sure that if you be doing this to me, you doing it to Mae and the kids too."

"Oda-Lee, do me a favor and do a lot of shutting up."

"I feel like there is something you ain't telling me, Jabo. You forget I have known you all my life. Now tell your sister what's wrong."

Anie was a terrible driver. One day while buying a car, she left the dealership and had two accidents before she even got home.

"I'll tell you if you take your foot off the damn gas pedal." Jabo sighed. "Charles finally moved out to his own house, but Mae and I just seem to have grown apart. She spends less and less time at home and don't pay no attention to Candy unless she screaming at her."

"Poor baby. I can tell she don't really have no connection to nobody," said Oda-Lee, shaking her head and only half-minding the road. "Have you tried talking to Mae about it instead of yelling at her or taking it out on me?"

"Oda-Lee, what you think, woman? Hell, yeah, I talked to her about it," said Jabo. "She say everything is fine, but I know there's something she don't want to tell me. I been living a loooong time and I know a cat, and I can damn sho always smell a rat."

"Jabo, what the hell you talking about?" They both started to laugh, and Betty shook her head, holding on for dear life as Oda-Lee sped down the freeway.

chapter 16

Bible Study, My Ass

Jabo started to wheel himself over to the phone but stopped halfway when it only rang once. "Damn. Who the hell playing phone games on a man with only one leg? That's just nasty, having me struggle all the way up and head to the damn phone so it just stop ringing." Jabo wheeled himself back to the TV. "What the hell you doing in there? Where you going now?" he yelled towards the bedroom, knowing full well Mae was in there getting ready to go out.

Mae stepped out of the bedroom. "Jabo, tonight is Wednesday and that means bible study," she said calmly.

"Bible study, my ass." He glared at her. "I ain't never seen no woman wear no low-cut dress to study no bible. Ya titties pretty much on the floor."

Mae merely looked down at the broken man who was once so strong and handsome.

Candy came crawling into the living room with her dolls, all ready for bed. "Momma...ouch." She pointed at her stomach.

Jabo smiled at her. "Where's your leg, Candy?"

"In room, Daddy. Hurts."

Mae frowned. "Damn, why does everything be hurting you?"

"Are you kidding me, Mae? This chile say she hurt, then as her mother you need to check her out and see what's wrong, not talk shit to her. I'm starting to think you ain't shit yo'self." Jabo looked at the sweet child in front of him, thinking about how much weight she had gained and how mistreated they both were.

"I know Jabo, yes, I know. I gotta make an appointment with Dr. Wright. Please remind me tomorrow. But now I gotta go." Mae continued getting herself ready for "church."

Jabo popped off his leg and when it hit the floor, Candy thought that was the funniest thing in the world and just laughed and laughed. He got down on the floor with her and started the chase, crawling after her. Excited, Candy moved as fast as she could and the two of them giggled and played like two babies on their knees. Jabo was one of the few people who ever showed Candy love, and she absolutely adored him.

Mae shook her head but smiled. "My God, will the two of you get out of the way? I'm trying to get dressed." She went off to do her makeup.

Jabo and Candy stopped their game and Candy lay down on the floor, out of breath. Jabo crawled over to Mae and looked up at her before she disappeared into the bathroom. "All right, when you get there, you be sure and thank God for sending me such a loving, faithful wife to take care of me during this trying time in my life." Mae looked down at him with a mixture of sadness and slight confusion. "What's wrong, babe? I'm serious. I know you doing all you can to make sure I'm taken care of. Going to church to pray and honor God is one of the ways you doing it," he said lovingly.

"That's the truth, Jabo, and I will give God thanks. These are hard times for all of us, but you know how much I love you," Mae replied, not sure if he was serious or not. "Don't you?"

"I don't know," he said, never taking his eyes off of her.

"I do, Jabo. You gotta know that. And you gonna make me late for bible study."

Ten minutes later she was out of the bathroom with a full face of makeup. She knocked on Peewee's door and opened it a crack. He tossed the magazine he was "reading" aside and ripped off the headphones. "Don't you knock?"

"I did, and who the hell you talking to like that? I'm going out. Keep an eye on your sister and Jabo for me and make sure if he need anything, you get it for him."

chapter 17

A Change of Seasons

M ore time went by, and the chronicles of a dysfunctional family were well underway. Jabo had become an unhappy shell of his former self, spending more and more time in bed. With his cancer progressing, not even Candy's smile or his favorite TV shows could inspire him to get himself up and ready to face the day. On the other hand, Mae was growing into the woman she had always wanted to be. Or at least she told herself she was, but what she was actually doing was spending more and more time out of the house, church being her go-to excuse just so she could get out and not have to deal with Jabo's decline.

She was so busy she clean forgot to take Candy to the doctor, even though the girl had complained of pain in her leg and stomach, and Jabo reminded her time and again. Perhaps she was "in denial" as they call it these days, or maybe she actually did forget. Even so, Candy was still as cute as any one-legged chocolate girl could be, but now several pounds too heavy for a babe her age. Most days she would spend next to Jabo's bed, drawing, playing with her dolls, or singing to herself. This entertained him and he always had a smile for his precious stepdaughter.

Peewee decided he'd had enough of small-town life and went off to NYC to join his older brother Gerry. Although Gerry was Mae's oldest son, people always thought they were brother and sister when they were younger. After Gerry had done his time in the Army, his good looks and spoiled attitude had driven him toward a life of hookers, drugs, sex, and crime, even though he could have gone off to college on the GI Bill.

Bonnie had almost entirely stopped coming over to the house at that point. Since Kevin wasn't there to take care of, Bonnie spent a lot of time over at the home of her "Latin lover." Betty got married and moved off to Atlanta, Georgia with her new husband, traveling and starting a new life. Incredibly enough, you can probably guess what his name was. As if we didn't have enough Willies in the family. I hope you're keeping track.

Let's recap. There was Peewee's and Candy's father Willie; there was Oda-Lee's crazy drunken ex-lover Mr. Willie; and now Betty had got herself a Willie. Willie Griffin was his name, and he was and always had been up to no good. In fact, he'd been in jail a couple times and although his crimes were misdemeanors, he began to think of himself as a hardened criminal and acted the part. The fact that he was working as a janitor didn't help his self-esteem, so when he and Betty met, he was ready to move out of New York and see if he could find something better in another state.

Oda-Lee wasn't happy about the union but what could she do? She tried to talk her out of it, but Betty was a grown woman and had to make her own mistakes. So life went on for her the same as it had. She was still driving like a crazy person and very active at her church, as always. While Betty taking off was just what the doctor ordered, there was a downside. Now that Betty was about of the house, Bonnie wasn't around, Mae was almost never home, and Oda-Lee was pretty much on-call when Jabo needed anything.

"Mae, can you bring me a glass of water?" Jabo yelled from the bedroom. "Mae! Where the hell are you?"

"She not here, Daddy," Candy said from her place on the floor.

"Yeah, I know she ain't here, sugar, I know." It was hard for him not to lose his patience with the girl, but he always managed to speak to her in loving tones. "How am I supposed to get to my doctor's appointment if yo momma ain't around?"

Candy smiled up at him, he down at her, then he grabbed the phone from the bedside table.

"Oda-Lee," he said before she had a chance to say hello, "I need to get to my appointment, and I don't know where that woman is. Oda-Lee, I'm telling you, she was supposed to be here, but every time I need something, she ain't nowhere to be found."

"She's probably just out getting some shopping done, calm your ass down."

"If she is, then it's with my money, that's fo damn for sure. Aw, hell, Oda-Lee, forget all of that, just come over here and help me get to the hospital."

"All right, I'll be right over."

"I'll tell you one thing, Oda-Lee, there ain't no way in hell I'm gon' sit round here and just let her do me any old kind of way, that's for sure." Jabo slammed the phone down and pulled himself up out of the bed and into his wheelchair. "Candy, go and get me my pants out the drawer, would you?"

Candy did as she was asked and crawled over to the dresser while Jabo mumbled to himself, "I wish I knew then what I know now. I would have left her ass right there in the ghetto. But I would have took you right with me."

* * *

"I'm trying to walk in, if you just hold the door open for me, Oda-Lee," Jabo fussed as he held onto the wall trying to make it inside the house.

"If you let me help you, then we can get you in, fool." Oda-Lee loved this man so much, and even underneath all the complaining and name-calling, it was plain that he loved her just as much.

"Mae, where you at?" Jabo yelled when they finally made it into the house.

Mae came running out of the kitchen to help him in the house with the wheelchair. "I'm right here, honey. Here's your chair, go on and sit on down," Mae said sweetly.

"Oh, sure, you being all nice as pie while Oda-Lee here, but before that you was telling me to kiss yo ass." He slammed back into the chair and wheeled himself over to the TV.

"I'm not feeling well, I think I need some milk or something," Oda-Lee said, following Mae into the kitchen.

"You want me to go and get you some?"

"Naw, girl, I'm just gonna get me that glass and go and lay in there on the couch for a minute until my stomach settles."

"I was just fixing dinner, you can stay for that if you feel better," Mae said and continued to do the cooking while Oda-Lee and Jabo watched some TV, Candy sitting at his feet.

"Damn, Jabo, what the hell is going on with this baby girl," Oda-Lee said when she saw Candy on the floor with her dolls. Even though she was smiling at the girl, inside her heart she felt a sharp pain. There was something seriously wrong, and she decided then and there that if Mae didn't take that child to see Dr. Wright soon, she was going to do it herself.

Dinner came and went. Oda-Lee and Mae did the washing up and then the two of them helped Candy with her bath and into bed. Oda-Lee went back to the couch to watch some more TV before she went home, but she ended up falling asleep. Mae covered her with a blanket then she and Jabo went into their room to get him undressed and ready for bed.

"Didn't you remember that I had a doctor's appointment today?" he asked.

"Yes, Jabo, I remembered, but you knew I had a hair appointment. I thought we were going to reschedule your doctor."

"Reschedule?! Are you serious, woman? You mean to tell me you would rather go get that nappy-ass shit combed to the front instead of making sure your husband is doing okay? I don't know what to think anymore, Mae."

"Jabo, I don't know what you mean. Anyway, it's ten thirty at night so just go to sleep," Mae said with an attitude.

This went on until finally Mae turned out the light, rolled over, and waited until she heard Jabo snoring.

The entire house was silent and completely dark when, around four in the morning, a sound like glass bottles crashing onto the floor rang out and the lights came on, catching Mae like a deer in headlights, trying to climb in the back window. Jabo was sitting there in his wheelchair, a shotgun pointed directly at her.

"I knew it, bitch! I knew it! Bonnie was right about you all along. Sneaking out when you think I'm asleep? How much lower can you go, woman?"

Mae stood there in shock until she realized that Jabo had lined up about thirty empty Coke bottles at the base of the window.

"I know you been cheating on me. The man who stood by you when everyone was telling me you were a low-life ho."

"Jabo, what the hell are you doing?" Oda-Lee ran into the kitchen after being woken up by the racket. "Look, baby, put the gun down, you don't want to do this. She sho ain't worth it." She gently took the gun out of his hand.

Jabo held back his tears as he turned his chair around to go back into the bedroom.

"Mae," Oda-Lee said firmly, "what the hell are you doing to my brother? After all the shit you went through with this family and me guiding you through it, just so you could end up making a fool of all of us?" Oda-Lee looked Mae in the face. "What's your problem, messing up a life like this...for what?" Mae dropped her head and didn't say a word, sinking down into one of the kitchen chairs. "I should have let him shoot your ass," Oda-Lee said angrily. "And take your daughter to the goddamn doctor, Mae." Oda-Lee walked out of the kitchen and down the driveway to her car.

After a while, Mae went and lay down on the couch, dreading the conversation she was going to have to have with Jabo.

chapter 18

New Family Members

"Daddy! Look who's here, Daddy. Daddy!?" Bonnie yelled, or I should say spoke in her normal, loud-ass voice as she stepped into the house with her entourage. "Daddy, where you at?"

Jabo came wheeling out of the bedroom, glasses crooked and with no shirt on. "What in the hell is your problem? It's six in the morning." By this time he was only a fraction of the man he used to be, although still a firecracker, ready to explode at any time. "And who the hell are all of these ugly-ass people you bringing into my house?" He locked the wheels on his wheelchair and fixed his glasses.

"Be nice, Daddy," Bonnie said. "This is Benny [I bet you thought his name was gonna be Willie] and these are his children Janet, Evelyn, and Lissette. Ain't they just the prettiest little things?"

"Yeah, but who the hell are they, a Puerto Rican singing group?"

"No, Daddy, Benny's my husband," Bonnie answered carefully.

"Husband! You done went and got married to this man and ain't tell nobody?"

"Daddy, we went to the Justice of the Peace."

"I don't care who the hell you went to. Get this ugly-ass man out of my house!" he yelled.

"Oh, but you can have that bitch and her nasty kids you brought into the family without asking anybody's opinion, can't you?" Bonnie said with her head held high.

"Get yo ass outta here!" Jabo started throwing everything within his reach towards her.

Mae came out of the bedroom pulling her bathrobe closed. "What the hell is going on out here?" she asked Jabo, half-asleep.

"Get your ass back into the bedroom," Jabo snapped. "This is all your fault anyway."

Mae did as she was told. It was going to be hard enough talking to him later, never mind getting involved in what was going down right now. She was already in the doghouse, so she was trying to keep the peace as much as possible.

"Daddy!" Bonnie yelled, running out of the house, shielding the girls from Jabo's projectiles.

"Me God, Me God!" Benny kept repeating as he fled Jabo's wrath. He only knew a few good words in English but had no idea where they were supposed to go in a sentence.

"And stay out!" Jabo yelled, rolling back into the bedroom. "Damn women gonna be the death of me, I swear to the Lord."

When Jabo got in the room, Mae was sitting on the edge of the bed, tears streaming down her face. "Jabo?"

He didn't answer her, just wheeled himself back over to his side of the bed and sat there, not moving, staring at the wall. He wasn't sure what to do with all the feelings going around inside him. At the bottom of it all, though, there was the love he still had for Mae, even though he wanted to kick her ass to Hell and back.

"Jabo," she said again, this time louder, "are you not going to talk to me for the rest of your life?"

"No, actually, I'm not going to talk to you for the rest of *your* life," he said.

"What is that supposed to mean, Jabo?"

"It means I'm going to kill yo ass if you do this to me again."

"Jabo, listen—"

"Don't you give me any of that 'Jabo listen' shit. I took yo ass in when everybody was talkin' about you and telling me I was making a mistake and still, because I love you, I decided to go ahead with it. I saw me in you is what I saw, and I was hoping we would both change our ways. I did. But you..." He trailed off, maybe thinking of the lost opportunities, perhaps just thinking how stupid he was to believe a ho could become a housewife.

"I know, Jabo, and I can't tell you how sorry I am and how much I appreciate—"

"You don't appreciate shit. You don't appreciate it. You waited right good until I got down to go back to your ways and find something else," Jabo said, tears filling his eyes. "You embarrassed me in front of my family, my friends, and most of all, myself. Right now I feel just like that stupid old man everyone always thought I was for dealing with you. You are nothing more than a two-dollar ho who owes me change."

Mae was speechless. There was nothing she could say. She knew he was right. Then, after what felt like a hundred years, Jabo turned to Mae and looked her in the eyes.

"I will give you one more chance to make things right, Mae, because this is the kind of man I am. I don't know who it is you running around with, and I don't even want to know, but if you have any decency, you will stop seeing him now and give me the chance to die in peace thinking that someone in this life really loved me."

Crying but trying to hold the sound back, Mae felt small and useless and ready to make things good with her man. "Jabo, I know you'll say that sorry didn't do it, but I really, truly am sorry I hurt you. I want to make a promise to you now that I will stop everything and that from here on out, I'll be here for you and Candy. I do now and I always will love you." Mae knelt down in front of Jabo in his wheelchair. "I will never forget what you did for me and my children, Jabo. Ever." She grabbed him around the waist and hugged him in his chair, harder than she ever had, and even though he didn't hug her back, he felt every bit of her pain.

"Okay, damn, Mae, let go. What you tryin' to do, strangle me? I'mma die soon enough."

Mae wiped away the last of her tears. She looked up at him and thought to herself, *What in the hell was I thinking, going off with another man?*

chapter 15

Crystal Beach

It was the Saturday after Jabo and Mae decided to give it another try, as well as having kicked Bonnie and her Latin lover out of the house at six in the morning, but because he was in a forgiving mood, and pushed slightly by Oda-Lee, Jabo decided to give Bonnie's new family a chance. Being benevolent all of a sudden, he told Oda-Lee he wanted to do something fun for everyone, kind of like a new start. Oda-Lee had a brilliant idea: she would plan a trip for the whole family to go out to the amusement park at Crystal Beach.

It was a place in high swing with rollercoasters, bumper cars, and the wonderful beach. Oda-Lee got free tickets through the church and told Jabo that they cost thirty-nine dollars, which she would then take and buy all his Christmas gifts with. She didn't see anything wrong with recycling gifts and shit.

As they were getting ready to leave, Mae said to Jabo, "By the way, I'm taking Candy to the doctor on Monday."

"It's about damn time! I don't know why you don't stay on top of her medical stuff. That girl should be your priority. Hell, even before me."

Mae knew he was right and there was no sense in defending herself.

* * *

"Hold on, hold on, I'm coming." Oda-Lee came running into the living room half-dressed to answer the phone. "Hello! How's my baby doing?"

"*I'm doing okay, Momma,*" Betty said on the other end.

"Oh no," Oda-Lee said immediately. A few months before, Betty had moved down to Atlanta with her husband Willie, and since then she'd only talked to her a few times, but she could hear loud and clear that something wasn't right.

"Wait a minute. If there is one thing in this world I know, it's my daughter, so I'm gonna ask you one more time. What's wrong with you, girl?"

"*I'm just missing the family, Momma, that's all.*"

"Are you sure? That man is treating you right, ain't he?"

"*Yes, Momma. Willie is okay.*"

"Okay? What the hell is that supposed to mean, Betty?" Silence. "Look, if there are any problems down there, you let me know and you can always come home, do you hear me? I will kick his ass myself if he ain't treating you right."

"*Yes, Momma, thank you,*" Betty said, clearly holding back tears.

"Betty, you know I love you and you can always come home, no questions asked. Don't you forget it."

"*Thank you, Momma, I gotta go.*" Betty hung up the phone.

"Betty! Betty!" Betty was gone. "Lord, protect my daughter," Oda-Lee said aloud. She looked at the clock on the wall. "Damn, I'm gonna be late!"

* * *

Oda-Lee pulled up in front of Jabo's house and honked three times before getting out to help everyone into their cars. Bonnie, Benny, and his three daughters climbed into the car with Oda-Lee, while Mae, Jabo, and Candy followed in Jabo's car.

Everyone was so excited about going, and they started the long hour-and-a-half ride to the theme park.

"What in the hell you following Oda-Lee for? You know she drive like a bat outta hell!" Jabo yelled as Mae drove carefully behind Oda-Lee, avoiding the potholes and trying not to upset Jabo, both of which were nearly impossible.

"She said she knew a shortcut to the park. And since I don't remember how to get there..." Mae said in the sweetest voice she could. She was still walking on eggshells, trying to make up for the fact that she had been creeping.

"What, and you think just 'cause I got one less leg I got me half a brain now and don't know how to get there?" Jabo said with a sly smile. But he put his hand on Mae's thigh to let her know he wasn't mad. He didn't want to be mad anymore, that was for sure.

"Momma! Can I go on the rides?"

"'Course you can, Candy, you can go on any ride you want."

"Yaaaaaay!"

Jabo smiled back at her. "Look at my little lady. You know your birthday coming up soon. What do you want for your birthday, Candy?"

"Daddy, I want whatever you get me." For a child that was mostly ignored or not given all of the special care and attention a child in her condition should get, she was nothing less than an angel.

* * *

"There it is!" Oda-Lee yelled, pointing to a sign that read:
CRYSTAL BEACH
10 MILES

"I told all y'all I know what I'm talkin' 'bout. I knew there was gonna be a quick way to get here." Oda-Lee gripped the steering wheel tight, gunning it to the finish line.

"Anie! Slow down!" Bonnie cried, holding on to the dashboard. "I don't wanna die today!"

"Quick, quick," Benny said in the back seat, trying to figure out the English words to say as he looked for the seatbelt.

Oda-Lee honked the horn as she pulled the big sedan into the parking lot, Mae carefully pulling up right next to her. They all started unloading out of the cars, and Mae helped Jabo out and into his wheelchair.

"I'm surprised we made it," Jabo said.

"You always got something to say. Just give me the tickets," Oda-Lee said. "Tickets?" Jabo echoed. "You said you was gonna get the tickets from church."

"Lord have mercy I did, and I thought I put them tickets right in my purse." Oda-Lee frantically checked her pockets.

"Oda-Lee, you had us come all the way out here to this damn park and you forgot to get the tickets!?" Jabo exclaimed, but half expecting it. "I should take my leg off and beat the hell outta you."

"No, uh, no. Is that no long, where, from—"

"Damn, Benny, shut the hell up till you learn how to speak English, boy," Jabo snapped at the poor guy while his girls hid behind their daddy's legs. "Just to show you what a prince I am, I will buy all the tickets again, but Oda-Lee, you gonna pay me back every dime."

Oda-Lee nodded and for once had nothing to say except, "Thank you, brother." She knew full well she would have to be paying nothing.

Mae wheeled Jabo over to the ticket counter so he could purchase the tickets, then they all went into the park, cursing and fussing and laughing, finally starting what was to be one of the best days the family had seen yet.

chapter 20

The Check-up

"Morning, Mae. Why you up so early?" Jabo asked, half-asleep, to his wife as she was getting dressed. Her back was to him and she didn't turn around or answer him. "Mae, what's wrong with you? You goin' deaf?"

"I'm sorry, I just....I just wanna make sure me and Candy get to the doctor in time."

Jabo could tell Mae was choking back tears so he decided to keep the snide comments to himself. He sat up in bed. "Baby, come on over here. What's wrong? I can hear you ain't right."

She went over to him, then started to cry and speak at the same time and nothing was understandable. "I'm just so worried about Candy. I know it looks like I don't care a lot of the time, but Jabo, all I am is worried and I just don't wanna face..." and then she started talking some kind of language that Jabo couldn't understand a word of since she was blubbering though her tears.

"What the hell you talking about, Mae? Can't nobody understand that Jap-talian. Stop and start again."

She got hold of herself and took a deep breath. "I think Candy has cancer."

"Why the hell you think that, hmm? Baby girl is sick, we all know that. She probably just needs another kind of medication to control that weight she been putting on," Jabo said, trying to comfort a clearly messed-up Mae.

"'Cause her stomach is swollen and hard and she's been sweating and feeling dizzy, and yesterday morning she threw up, and she ain't never done that before except when she was a baby."

"There ain't no sense getting all worked up over what ain't yet happened, but whatever it is, Mae, we'll deal with it, that's for sure."

"Thank you, baby. I love you." She kissed him and walked out of the room to go and get Candy ready for the visit to the doctor.

* * *

Mae opened the door to Dr. Wright's office with Candy holding tightly onto her hand. Dr. Wright was the first African-American pediatrician in Buffalo, so pretty much everybody who was black went to Dr. Wright. Mae spotted Miss Aletha, who was sitting in the waiting room with her daughter Rene. Everyone in the neighborhood always looked at them as the ugliest people that had ever walked the face of the earth. People used to refer to them as "Grape Ape and Child." Yes, I know, mean as hell, but there you have it. She was mean half the time anyway, so people didn't feel bad calling her names.

"Hey, M-M-Mae, how are you?" Letha stuttered. Yeah, on top of everything else, the poor lady stuttered and also had a lisp, along with an annoying sort of tic. Basically, she was just fucked up.

"Hey, Letha, how you doin'?" Mae was not in the mood for Letha, but what could she do?

"G-G-Girl, I'm fine. Jus' bringin' Rene in here to get her ch-ch-check-up before the summer is over and everyone is c-c-coming before the after-effects of school."

No one ever questioned Miss Aletha, even though most of the time they had no idea what the hell she was talking about. Like now.

"Lela Carter," the nurse called loudly into the waiting room. Mae was delighted that her conversation with Miss Aletha would be cut short so she wouldn't have to struggle through with interpretation.

"Letha, honey, I'll see you later." Mae hurried away with Candy.

"O-kkkkkay, M-M-Mae, ta-ta-ta-talk to you lat—"

Mae shut the door before she even heard the last of what Miss Aletha was saying.

"Hello there, Miss Carter," the nurse said. "And hello there to you, beautiful little lady."

Candy smiled that sweet smile and replied shyly, "Hi."

"The name's Burder, don't you remember? I've been married for a while now," Mae said, slightly testy because she'd had to correct her so many times before.

"Oh, I am sorry, that's right. Forgive me. Well, I'm just going to take Lela's temperature and get her ready for Doctor Wright." She sat Candy on the table, put a thermometer in her mouth, and checked her heartbeat. "Seems fine. Dr. Wright will be with you in a moment." She left quickly, fidgeting and seeming a bit uncomfortable, possibly because this was the fifth time she had forgotten Mae's last name.

"Momma, I want to go home."

"Girl, we just got here. We gonna wait until you been seen, then we'll go home, okay?" Mae was trying to hide her anxiousness, but Candy could sense it and didn't push, wanting to save her mother from having to get mad or anything.

"Okay, Momma."

"If you're good, we can stop at McDonald's and get you a Happy Meal."

Dr. Wright came into the office. "Hello, Missus Burder. How are you and Lela doing today?"

"We're doing just fine, but I sure am worried about some things. Her stomach is so hard, maybe we need to take some tests and—"

Dr. Wright smiled warmly. "Missus Burder, I understand your concern, but I'm the doctor here." Mae instantly calmed down. Dr. Wright had that way about her. "Everything's going to be fine, don't worry. I'm going to have a good look, then have the nurse come back and take some blood."

"That sounds great," Mae said, relieved, and let Dr. Wright do what she did best.

She took out her penlight and looked into Candy's mouth and ears, then checked her heart and chest with the stethoscope, asking all the usual questions.

"Does this hurt?"

"Do you have regular bowel movements?" (Candy had to ask her momma what that meant before she could answer.)

"Do you have trouble sleeping?"

Dr. Wright was slightly taken aback to hear that Candy had started her period so early, and after asking why Mae hadn't brought the girl in sooner, she asked about her periods, like when they started, how many she'd had, and if her tummy hurt a lot when she was menstruating. When she was done, she sat across from Mae and Candy.

"Lela's heartbeat sounds like she may have a bit of a murmur. I'm hearing a sort of an echo or something like that. Not alarming, but I would like to have a closer look. Her stomach worries me as well, but I don't want to speculate until we have test results. Once we do, we'll go from there. For now, I want the nurse to make an appointment with a heart specialist at Buffalo General and get her looked at as soon as possible."

"Thank you, Doctor Wright," Mae said.

"Thank you, Doctor Wright," Candy repeated.

"You are both very welcome, and Lela, because you were such a good girl, Marina is going to give you a lollipop. Okay?"

"Okay!" Candy had a look of sheer delight. She was so easy to please, that girl.

"Missus Burder, we'll call you as soon as the tests come in and set up an appointment."

THE CHECK-UP

After Dr. Wright left the examination room, Mae and Candy gathered their things and walked back out into the waiting room. Miss Aletha was still there, her mouth wide open, snoring like a grizzly bear. Mae waved at Rene and tiptoed past her mother, excited she wouldn't have to talk to her again.

chapter 21

The Birthday Party, Part Two

With nothing to do now but wait for the results of Candy's tests, a hot August week went by, and Mae and Jabo settled into a love/hate sort of groove, with Mae being on her best behavior. She had plenty to do and kept herself busy with the preparations for Jabo's birthday. Not knowing if he would see another one, Mae wanted to make it special. She thought she'd get back in on his good side, so she made sure everything was just how he liked it.

The morning started off normal enough. In fact, Jabo thought it was too normal for having a birthday. Still, he was running out of energy to argue about things he couldn't do anything about, so he stayed in bed for most of the morning, watching TV and expecting Mae to come in with breakfast in bed or something. She did bring him some coffee, then said she was going out for a while, and he wondered if she'd forgotten his birthday altogether.

"Where the hell yo momma go this time, child? She know it's my birthday!" Jabo asked Candy, who was hanging out in the living room with him as she always did.

"Yeah, Daddy, she know."

The front door opened and closed. "Mae? That you?" he called.

Mae popped her head around the corner. "Jabo, can you come into the dining room? I need your help with something." She smiled sweetly, then disappeared.

Wheeling himself out into the living room, he was muttering to himself something about why the hell his own wife wasn't all over him on his birthday and that nobody gave two shits about him. When he came round the corner into the dining area saying to Mae, "What the hell is it, woman?" he was drowned out by a loud, "*Surprise!*"

There stood his entire family around the table, in the middle, his favorite kind of cake, German chocolate. They all began to sing "Happy Birthday," and Jabo got the biggest smile. When they were finished and he started to applaud, the group moved aside and there appeared a tall figure.

"Hey there, old man." Kevin approached Jabo and knelt down in front of his wheelchair.

"Boy, what the hell you..." He couldn't finish his sentence because he broke down crying, weeping in a way none of them had ever seen.

"Daddy, don't cry or you gonna make me cry!" Bonnie yelled in her speaking voice.

"I'm going in the kitchen to wipe these tears and then cut this cake. Hell, I didn't spend all night cooking this damn thing from scratch so that y'all come cryin' over it and not eat it," Oda-Lee said.

Everyone laughed, and Jabo continued to hug Kevin. "You just made my birthday, boy."

"I'm lucky I got me a weekend leave from the base. I convinced them to let me come, you know, 'cause I didn't want to miss your birthday," Kevin said, without saying he told them it might be his last.

"You did the right thing, Kevin, boy," Oda-Lee said before going into the kitchen.

"Let's get this party started!" Bonnie began pouring people drinks before the candles on the cake were even lit while someone went and put some music on.

* * *

The next morning Mae went into the kitchen to start cleaning up after the party. Pretty much everyone except for Oda-Lee had stayed over because they almost drank themselves to death, so there were bodies sleeping on wherever they could find a spot. Benny was in one of the armchairs and Bonnie was in the other, Kevin laid out on the couch. He was just waking up when Candy came out of her bedroom.

"Hey, Candy girl, come on over here," he whispered to her.

"Momma!" Candy shrieked, and began to crawl as fast as she could into the kitchen.

"Girl, what is wrong with you?"

"He's getting up, he can see me," Candy said with panic in her eyes.

"Damn, girl. That's Kevin. I know you haven't seen him a while but that's sure enough him."

Kevin walked into the kitchen. "Morning," he said, passing by Mae and Candy, like saying it took all he had.

"Momma." Trembling, Candy held tight to her mother's leg.

"Damn, girl, what the hell is wrong with you?"

Kevin left out the back door, letting the screen door slam shut behind him.

"Candy, you stop acting up. Go back in there and play."

"Okay, Momma," Candy said, sobbing.

When she left the kitchen, the telephone rang. "Hello? Oh, hello there, Doctor Wright, how are you? Yes, I'm listening." Mae sat down, beginning to feel a bit uneasy.

Bonnie entered the kitchen, looking like something the cat had drug in, and walked straight out the back door without saying a word.

Right when Mae hung up the phone, Jabo wheeled into the kitchen and saw the look on her face.

"What is it? Who was that on the phone?"

"That was Doctor Wright. She said we gotta come in. She wanna talk to us about Candy and what our options are."

"What the hell? Why didn't she tell you now what the hell is wrong? Damn, Mae, you shoulda—"

"Shoulda what, Jabo? Told the doctor how to do her damn job? We go in tomorrow and then we'll know more." She was on the verge of tears. "I know she must be about to die, Jabo. Why else would she not want to tell me on the phone?"

Jabo wheeled himself over to her and took her hands. "Listen, Mae, everything is going to be okay. All we gotta do is say a prayer and move forward. It's all gonna be fine, you'll see." Mae didn't respond. "Mae, did you hear what I said?"

"Yes, Jabo, I heard you," Mae said. "I know you're right, she'll be okay. Let's just talk about something else, okay?" Mae looked up at him with a defeated expression. "I'm gonna go and get Candy's favorite pancake mix, I know she'd love that." She bolted up out of her chair and grabbed her car keys, then exited the house.

"What am I going to do about your momma?" Jabo asked Candy when he went back into the living room where that round chocolate child was as happy as could be, sitting on the floor playing with her dolls with a cartoon playing on the TV in the background.

"I don't know, Daddy...bite her?" Candy said and the two of them burst out laughing, then Jabo started to chase Candy around the room with his wheelchair.

As you now know, Jabo and Candy had a bond that was stronger than anyone else's in the family. Maybe their condition had a lot to do with it. God has a funny way of taking care of his own, putting people in your path that sometimes need you as much as you need them, or replacing someone you thought should be loving you with one who will love you even more.

"There she go, that's my little girl right there," Jabo said as Candy crawled along the living room floor, smiling when she went past his wheelchair, then plopped down on the floor and continued to play with her dolls. Jabo smiled with glee like a proud father who had just seen his child for the first time.

The back door opened, and the screen door slammed shut. "Mae is that you? Come on in here."

Mae came in and stood behind Jabo's wheelchair. "What is it, Charles?"

"What in the hell did you just say to me?" Jabo turned his head and raised his voice as high as he could get it these days.

"I said what's the matter, Jabo?"

"Bitch, you called me Charles. What the hell you calling me Charles for, Mae?""Jabo, I'm sorry, it was a mistake. Anyway, what's wrong?"

"That ain't no mistake. You think I'm stupid, huh? Do you?" He whipped around and the chair almost knocked her over while Candy crawled into a corner and tried to protect herself with one of her dolls.

"Can you stop, Jabo? It wasn't nothing, only a simple mistake."

He didn't think so at all and wheeled past her in a rage, forgetting what he had called her in there for in the first place.

Mae went over to Candy and saw she was sitting in a pool of blood. She quickly got her into the bathroom. "Does it hurt, baby?"

"No, Momma, it doesn't hurt. What's wrong with me?"

"I don't know, but Doctor Wright is gonna tell us tomorrow. We gonna get you all cleaned up then have some breakfast, okay?"

"Okay, Momma."

Mae put Candy back with her dolls so she could calm Jabo down and go and make them some breakfast. But it was impossible; Jabo would not be calmed down.

"I know what you doing, and I'm going to shoot the both of you dead!" he yelled.

"You don't know nothing, Jabo, I am not, and I would never mess around with a member of your own family!" Mae screamed back at him. "I don't have to take this. No, I do not." Mae stormed out the kitchen door, over to her car, and pulled away.

Candy came crawling into the kitchen, crying her eyes out. "Momma, don't leave me!" It was too late.

She and Jabo stood there looking at the door. Then Jabo wheeled close and put his arms around her. "Hush, Candy. Hush baby, I'm here. I know you want your Momma, but don't you worry, I will never leave you." He knew he was making a promise he could never keep.

She looked up and smiled at him through her tears. "Thank you, Daddy, I love you."

"I love you too, Candy," Jabo said as he stroked her hair. "How about I try and make those pancakes, hm?"

She looked up at him with glistening eyes and her thousand-watt smile.

chapter 22

Denny's

While the drama over at Mae and Jabo's was playing out, Oda-Lee was having some of her own. She was just getting back from the morning mass at church when there was a knocking at her door.

"Who the hell is that at the door? I know ain't nobody decided to drop by my house without calling first," Oda-Lee fussed. "Who's there?" No answer, only the incessant knocking. "Okay, I got twenty-two reasons why you better identify yourself," she said, then peeked through the crack, leaving the chain still on the door. "Lord have mercy, what the hell you doing here?" Oda-Lee cried out as Betty and Willie yelled, "Surprise!"

"Why didn't you tell me y'all were coming? I would have cooked and had everybody here to see you."

"Which is exactly why we didn't tell you we were coming," Betty said with a hint of sarcasm. "We just coming for a couple days. Willie needed to see his dad and we thought we'd stop by."

"Stop by?" Oda-Lee jerked her head back with an attitude. "I ain't see you in God knows how long and you think you just gon' *stop by*?"

Her voice went from baritone to soprano, ending in the highest pitch her voice could produce.

"Hello, Momma, how are you?" Willie said with open arms.

Oda-Lee put her hands on her hips. "I'd rather you call me Anie as I still ain't sure I don't have ta whip yo ass about my daughter yet, and it would be a shame to disown my own son, now wouldn't it?"

"Okay, Anie, I'm sorry." Willie grinned and gave her a hug.

"Come on in the house and bring all your stuff in this back bedroom. I'm gonna put something on the stove."

Oda-Lee disappeared into the kitchen, pots rattling.

"Momma," Betty called after her, knowing it was useless trying to protest, "you don't have to go through all of that!"

Oda-Lee came back out from the kitchen. "Hell, I'm about to make y'all some grits and eggs 'cause I haven't gone shopping and I ain't got a drop of food in the house."

"Willie, take this stuff in the back," said Betty. "I'm gonna help Momma."

"Momma? Why you don't have to call her Anie?" Willie asked Betty.

"For the same damn reason you shouldn't be calling yo wife momma," Oda-Lee scolded. "She ain't yo momma."

"I know that, Anie, that's just an expression cats use with the ladies, you know," Willie said, attempting to school Oda-Lee.

"Chile, I know what the hell it mean. I wasn't asking for an answer. Folks been sayin' that for years, you ain't found somethin' new. Boy, you don't know nothin', do you?" She shook her head with a slight grin, knowing that she had used him, and also knowing he would be scared to go toe-to-toe with her, even if she was wrong. "Well I do, and I know I will kill anyone who messes with my girl." Oda-Lee looked over the top of her glasses that had slid down on her lightly sweaty nose. "You got that?" she asked, holding a dull butter knife in one hand and an almost empty glass milk bottle in the other.

"I'll be in the bedroom taking a nap if anyone needs me," Willie said, hurrying into the back room.

"Momma, you just scared my husband," Betty said, not knowing if that was a good thing or not.

"Girl, if a butter knife and a bottle of milk gonna scare that man, then he don't deserve to be nobody's husband. I should have done more than I did."

"What are you talking about, Momma?"

"Betty, I know you like the back of my own hand. You are my daughter," Oda-Lee said.

Betty turned her back and pretended to be fidgeting with the silverware on the table so Oda-Lee wouldn't see her face. "But, Momma, I'm...Momma, I'm..." Betty couldn't finish her sentence for fear Oda-Lee was going to yell or speak loud enough for Willie to hear.

"You're not going back to Georgia, are you?" Oda-Lee asked Betty.

Betty looked at her with amazement. "Momma, how did you know what I was going to say?"

Oda-Lee leaned in close. "Betty honey, I seen that bruise on your arm and I know you didn't get that from walking into no doorknob. Besides that, it looks like you brought your whole damn closet with you. If Willie didn't notice anything after that, then that man is as dumb as he is blind."

Betty smiled, a tear streaming down her face.

"Listen, you are my child and you will always be my child. I'mma cook up a hot pot of grits and dare that nigga to say one word!"

Betty started to cry.

"Don't you worry, honey. Hush. It's all gonna be okay. I'll make the cheap grits. From the dollar store, not the Quaker ones." They both laughed. "Don't worry, honey, Momma got this. We gonna figure out the perfect plan."

They sat down at the table and Betty took her mother's hand.

"I'm so afraid to tell him," Betty said fearfully.

"Don't be. I'm here. He been treating my daughter wrong, so the only thing he gonna leave here with is three shoes. Two on his feet and one in his ass!"

* * *

After she dried her tears, Betty went into the bedroom to see if Willie was still napping and saw him sitting on the edge of the bed, just waking up.

"Damn, girl, yo momma, she don't like me. She been talkin' shit to me since we walked in the door. I think we better go on our way."

"Willie, I'm not going back to Atlanta with you," Betty said after mustering all her courage. "I'm gonna stay here with Momma."

"Say what?" Willie jumped up off the bed, ready to go from zero to a hundred. "What in the hell are you talking about, you not coming back home with me?"

"Willie, calm down. I just thought it would be best if I stayed up here with Momma for a while. She needs me."

"She don't need you! I need you!" Willie started yelling and flailing his arms. Betty started to get nervous, but still tried to calm him down. "You ain't staying here no way. What you are going to do is get yo ass up and get ready and we are going to get the hell outta here in fifteen minutes."

"Willie, please, I think you're being—" Betty tried to interject.

Willie raised a hand. "I don't give a flying f—aaaaaaaahhhhhhh!" He screamed at the top of his lungs as the hot grits burned into his skin. Willie fell to the floor and began rolling around, trying to figure a way out.

"I—told—you—not—to—mess—with—my—daughter!" Oda-Lee hit him with the pot with every word. "Now get all your shit and get the hell out of my house, you bastard," Oda-Lee said, giving him a small chance to gather his composure.

"Both of y'all are crazy, you deserve each other." Willie ran out of the bedroom to go wash the grits off his back.

"Momma, I can't believe you just did that!"

"I knew that nigga was gonna try some funny business, so I kept the pot simmering and ready."

Oda-Lee and Betty collected Willie's things. Eventually he came out of the bathroom but was scared to get his stuff out of the bedroom, so he stood in the hallway and looked from Oda-Lee to Betty, waiting for one of them to say something.

"You got ten seconds to get all two of yo raggedy-ass suitcases and get the hell out of my house, bastard, or I got a fresh pot with no butter in it waiting."

He was so scared of that woman, Willie ran out the door, leaving his shoes. Oda-Lee ran after him and threw them out the door. "And take these old run-down flops with you!"

"What am I gonna do with you, Momma?" Betty said, embracing her mother.

"You gonna love me half as much as I love you, baby, that is all you gotta do. Better to have no man in the house than a low-down, good-for-nothin' fool like that one. Come on girl, let's go to Denny's and get something to eat, I lied about having more grits."

* * *

"Where you wanna sit, Momma?" Betty asked.

"We gonna sit at the window. I hate sittin' with my back to the door. Something happen in the restaurant, I need to see who I gotta fight," Oda-Lee said and they both laughed. One thing Oda-Lee could do was make people laugh. Almost as much as she could make them cry.

"Right this way," said the hostess, leading them to their seat. Just before they got to the last seat in the row, Oda-Lee heard a familiar voice.

"Charles, we gonna have to stop. I love you so much, but what happened at home this morning, I can't go through that again, we gotta..."

Oda-Lee stopped in her tracks and turned to find Mae and Charles sitting in the same booth, on the same side. "Well, well, well. I didn't expect to see either of you here all hugged up in the corner."

"Oda-Lee, now you wait a minute. I'm just sitting here having breakfast with Charles."

"Right. *You* might be having breakfast, but it looks like he's all ready for dessert." "Aw, come on Anie, it's nothing like that. You know I'm not going to do nothing to Jabo like that."

Charles started to speak up but thought better of it when he looked at the two faces staring down at them. Betty's was full of knowing that they were lying, and that her mother would be going off in three, two, one—

"Both of you should be ashamed of yourselves!" Oda-Lee screamed. "That man has done nothing but help you both and this is the thanks you give him?"

"Keep your voice down, Momma!"

"Not a chance, Betty. I'll be damned if I'm going to stand here and watch my brother's wife and his nephew denounce his kindness and make him out to be an ass behind his back."

The patrons of Denny's were all ears and eyes, watching the soap opera unfold with great interest.

"There he is, sitting in a house that he pays all the bills for and makes sure to keep food on the table, even though he only got one leg and he's in pain and has less years to live than we all know. Y'all ought to be *ashamed,* I'm telling you. He took care of both of y'all. I'm not gonna let this happen. I'm gonna go and tell him, although I'm gonna give you a chance to tell him first. You got about as long as it's gonna take me to eat my damn French toast."

Everyone waited for a moment to make sure Oda-Lee was done.

"Oda-Lee, you are jumping to conclusions, and your jumping is going to cause more problems, as if we don't have enough of them right now." Mae got up and walked toward the door, Charles following close behind.

"Girl, I don't know who you think you fooling. I may look dumb to you, but one plus one has always come up the same number in my book, with yo lyin', cheatin' ass!" Oda-Lee yelled after them, then sat down in the booth where the hostess was going to seat them, smiling at the waiter as if she had just come from Sunday service. "Sit down, shuga. We are ready to order, young man. How are you today, doll?"

He looked confused but nodded. "I'm well, thank you."

"Momma," Betty said, shaking her head, "you are something else."

"Wait till I get to Jabo. I'm gonna be something else for sure." Oda-Lee took a sip of the coffee. "You just wait. My brother deserves better."

chapter 23

Surprise!

Later that evening, Jabo and Mae were discussing the situation in the only way they knew how. Yelling. Mae decided to head off Oda-Lee by telling Jabo herself that she and Charles had been seen at Denny's.

"I don't know what you think this is, Mae. I know you better than you think I do!"

"I'm telling you, Jabo, there was nothing more than us eating at the restaurant. I was upset and needed someone to talk to. I'm telling you this, honey, so that you will hear it from me and not secondhand."

"First of all, stop calling me honey. Second, the only reason you're telling me is because you done got caught. And third, you's a goddamn lie!"

He wheeled himself into the living room when the doorbell rang. Before he even got to the door, Oda-Lee burst in with Betty running behind her.

"Look, Jabo, I'm going to say it right out and you know I don't hold no punches," Oda-Lee said.

"I have been holding punches all day and a can of whoop-ass with Mae's and Charles's names written all over it," Jabo said.

"Both of you are wrong!" Mae yelled, but she was starting to get the feeling her protesting was useless.

"Wrong? How in the hell—" Jabo screamed.

"I know exactly what—" Oda-Lee said at the same time.

The two of them were yelling and screaming so loud Mae couldn't get a word in. Through the arguing and yelling and accusing, they heard a scream that sent them all running to the back of the house.

"Candy, what's wrong?" Oda-Lee asked with concern, being the first to reach the child, and also not thinking that maybe all that bickering and fighting was having a negative effect on that poor child.

"My stomach hurt bad!" Candy screamed. Mae leaned in and lifted her up off the bed and saw a pool of blood. By the amount of it, it wasn't period blood.

"Call 911!" Mae shouted and Betty ran to the phone.

"What happened to you, babe? What's going on?" Oda-Lee asked when Candy screamed in pain.

Mae wrapped her in the comforter and took her to the front of the house.

"I'm going with her," said Jabo.

"It's gonna be too hard to get you in that ambulance," Oda-Lee said to him. "Let's go in the car and meet them at the hospital."

"Shit, Oda-Lee, the way you drive...by the time we get there the girl gon' be dead," Jabo said, disappointed with just the thought of riding with her. "And this shit ain't over, Mae," he added, glaring at her as she opened the door for the rescue squad.

The EMT workers put Candy on a stretcher and as they carried her to the ambulance, Mae was next to Candy, answering their questions. "We just got some tests done and were waiting on the results, but because of her condition we expected some complications."

"We'll get her to Children's Hospital as soon as possible," an EMT said. Mae got in the back and he shut the door behind her. The rest of the family jumped in Oda-Lee's car and took off, heading to Children's Hospital.

* * *

"We're definitely going to the right place, Oda-Lee, because the way you drive, we definitely gone need to see the doctor when we get there," Jabo said from the back of the car.

"You right about that, Jabo. 'Cause even though you ain't no child, you act like it sometimes. Letting that ho into your house was one of the most childish things I ever seen in my life, and still I stuck by you and tried to help you make it work. But at least it brought Candy to us 'cause I don't know what would have happened to that child had she not been here." Oda-Lee's speech had some truth to it, but Candy would still be considered neglected in a lot of people's eyes.

They pulled up to the emergency room of Children's Hospital and got out of the car, rushing into the waiting room.

"Ma'am, you can't park your car at the entrance," a security officer said, standing in their way. Oda-Lee acted like she didn't even hear him and rolled on past him with Jabo's wheelchair. "I said you can't leave your car there!" Betty shrugged and followed her mother and Jabo. "Fine. I'll just have the damn thing towed then," the guard said under his breath.

Oda-Lee turned around and walked calmly back to the man, leaving Jabo in his chair between the inside and the outside, and said in the calmest voice possible, "With everything I have been through today, if I come out here and my car is gone, I'll break my foot off in yo ass." She turned and just went right back to pushing the chair.

"All right, well, don't leave it out here all day," he said, resigning himself to Oda-Lee's wrath.

When they entered the waiting room, they didn't see Mae and assumed she was in the room with Candy.

"We're looking for Lela Carter and Mae Burder," Jabo said to the lady at the reception.

"They are in with the doctor, sir. Please have a seat over there and we will contact—"

"You will let me go in there now! That's my wife and my daughter in there and I'm not waiting till you get in contact with nobody. Mae! Mae!"

"Sir, please, this is a hospital," the nurse said.

"Yes, and I also know it ain't no damn library, so if you don't take me back to where my family is, you are going to be needing every doctor in here for yourself."Mae came out from the back. "Jabo! What in the Lord's name are you doing?"

"You all have to be quiet, or I will have you escorted out," the nurse said just as the doctor came out into the waiting area.

"Missus Burder, please come in this way."

Jabo wheeled himself right behind them, and the others followed.

"Look, just tell us, is the baby okay?" Oda-Lee asked.

"I have asked Missus Burder to come back," the doctor said. "The rest of you, please wait—"

Oda-Lee had had enough. "We are not going anywhere until you tell us this baby is okay and that the tumor can be removed," she said sternly.

"Please listen carefully, and then Missus Burder and I really must get back to Lela. We have some good news and also some bad. Lela does not have a tumor. Although she will need plenty of rest and care, she will be fine," the doctor said reluctantly. "However...Lela is in labor."

There was a brief stunned silence. Jabo was the first to speak.

"Doctor, what the hell are you talking about? She only eleven years old."

"Yes, Mister Burder, this is very true. Yet, the fact remains that Lela Carter is with child and is soon going to be a mother. I need to take Missus Burder back with me so she can be there with her daughter when she gives birth."

"Let's go, doctor," Mae said, ignoring the others. She followed him to the back and everyone else went back into the waiting room.

* * *

For a while no one said anything, which was a miracle in and of itself. Someone went and got some sodas and chips to keep them occupied for what was probably going to be a long wait. After about twenty minutes, Betty said, "So let me get this straight, Candy is having a baby?"

"This is just about as crazy as I ever seen," Oda-Lee said, shaking her head in disbelief.

"At least she ain't got cancer, so I'm relieved," Jabo said, trying to look on the bright side. He sipped on a Coke and crunched on a bag of Bar-B-Q Fritos.

"What in the hell you talking about 'relieved'? Sittin' there sippin' on a Coke with yo long-ass lips. This just brings about more questions," Oda-Lee said.

"Questions like what, Oda-Lee? We just glad the baby isn't sick," Jabo muttered.

"Questions like who the hell the father of this child is, Jabo. Or do you think it's okay that someone raped that poor, defenseless baby?" Oda screamed.

"Momma!" Betty hissed. "Keep your voice down before they throw us out of this hospital."

"I'm sorry, honey, but this don't sit right with me at all. I think we should get—"

Mae came running in, grinning widely. "I'm a grandmother. Candy just gave birth to a eight-pound, seven-ounce beautiful baby boy."

Everyone spoke at once as they processed the news.

"How wonderful!" (A stranger)

"Oh. My. God. Yes." (Betty)

"Praise the Lord." (Jabo)

"Jesus help us all." Oda-Lee almost fainted, holding on to Betty.

"I couldn't be more confused about all of this, though." Mae sat down and shook her head.

"I know how you feel, Mae. I was confused when our family dog Pepe had puppies one winter even though she'd been locked up in the house with us the whole year. I guess God works in—"

"Jabo, shut the hell up. We ain't talking about no damn dog. This is serious," Oda-Lee snapped. "Mae, how is Candy baby doing?"

"She's doing fine, all things considered."

"When can we see my baby?" Jabo asked, dropping chips all over his lap.

"They have to run some tests first, and Candy needs some rest. They will both be released in a few days."

"I think we all should call it a night and wait until they are released," Oda-Lee said, grabbing her purse.

"Oh Lord, you telling me I gotta wait to see my baby?"

"Yes, Jabo, and I'm going to stay in here with her for the night. Let Oda-Lee take you home and you get some rest."

"Lord have mercy. Here we go again, back to the races," Jabo said.

"Well, you can wheel your ass all the way there too, Jabo," said Oda-Lee as they gathered their things and left the waiting room, each of them concerned with their own thoughts about the new, bouncing baby boy. "And why the hell you keep calling that child yo baby, Jabo?" Oda-Lee wheeled him out the door, crunching over a lonely Frito he'd left on the floor.

part two

chapter 24

The Baby Shower

The decorations were up at the house, and Oda-Lee was excitedly taping and blowing up balloons, laughing and giving out orders like she was talking through a megaphone.

"Unless you the father...and you better not be telling me that you is..." She stood there with a slight smile because she knew ain't no way in hell Jabo was the father of this baby. And although she loved Candy dearly, she feared the baby was going to be a freak, coming from that poor misfit of a girl.

"I'm just glad that baby is healthy and on his way home," Oda said to Jabo while she put the finishing touches on a German chocolate cake. "Anything could have happened to that child, but God saw fit to deliver him right to our wonderful care because—"

At exactly that moment the lock on the back door turned, and Mae came into the house holding the baby in one arm and Candy's hand with her free one. "Hello, everyone! We're home!"

Even Bonnie came running, calling out to some of the people in the living room, who all came in to get a look at the miracle baby.

119

I say "miracle" because up until now, there was no sign of anyone being the father, and people were more taken by the fact that Candy could even *have* a baby, so the other small details, like who the father was, could wait.

"I cannot tell you how so excited I am to see that child. Come to Anie, little man." Oda-Lee reached for the baby.

Mae moved the blue blanket away that was covering the baby's face and there I was.... It was the first time I looked out into the world to see all these ugly-ass people I didn't choose and who didn't choose me. My family.

"Oh my goodness, this is one of the most beautiful babies I have ever seen," Betty said with tears in her eyes.

"Yeah, he cute," Bonnie said reluctantly.

"Bring him over here so I can hold him," Jabo said with his frail arms extended.

Mae placed me carefully in Jabo's arms for the first time, and even though I was too young to remember, I somehow knew the love he had for me was one of a kind, and I'd soon find out it wouldn't be felt across the board. Whatever the case, I smiled at him as if I had just seen the sun rise for the first time.

Jabo looked up at Mae and over at Candy, who still hadn't really grasped the truth of what was happening in her world. "He got your smile, Candy. And hell, I will be damned if that boy doesn't look just like me," Jabo laughed.

"Momma, I miss my dolls. Can I go get them?" Candy asked, but her request fell on deaf ears. Everyone was focused on the baby.

"He don't look nothing like you, Daddy," Bonnie said. "He better not!"

"You right, Jabo, he looks just like you. First glance, honey, I see it. You ain't the only one he looks like," Oda-Lee said, standing in the middle of the kitchen.

All of a sudden it was so quiet you could hear a rat piss on cotton. Unlike moments before, this was what everyone wanted to know. Who the hell was the daddy of this special boy?

"Well, Oda-Lee? Who else you think he look like?" Miss Johnson from down the road asked. She had twenty children and none of them had the same father.

"I'm not sure who this baby looks like," Bonnie said, leaning in to the child to get a better look.

Oda-Lee watched Bonnie from the top of her glasses. "I'm telling you right here and now, it don't matter who he looks like, honey. This is June's baby."

"You's a lie! That would mean..." Bonnie stopped talking when she realized she had just called Anie a liar.

"Who the hell you calling a lie, Bonnie?" Oda-Lee slapped the hell out of Bonnie. Everyone started laughing, and the slap hurt her pride more than her head. "All y'all shut the hell up. If you make my boy cry, I'm going to have to whip every ass in here."

Everyone laughed again and went into the living room, turning the music loud. Bonnie slid out the side door when no one was looking. Thankfully, nobody noticed.

Boy-oh-boy, I was only in the world five days and the division and controversy was just getting started, me now being the only blood link between those two families who hated each other. I had no idea that I should have been on my knees before I could even crawl. Lord help me.

* * *

I'm lounging in the car seat on the picnic table while Momma (actually Mae, but just so you know, I call her Momma) is taking the clothes off the line, singing, *"Jesus is on that mainline, tell Him what you want. Jesus is on that mainline...."* when Bonnie comes barging into the backyard and getting all up in Mae's face.

"What the hell is your problem and who the hell do you think you are, bringing that damn baby into this family, acting like it's Kevin's?" Bonnie said, then snatched a white sheet off the line and slammed it into the mud.

"Look, Bonnie," Mae said, a river of rage seething beneath her calmness, "I never said that baby was Kevin's, Oda-Lee did. So if you got a problem with that, take it up with her." Momma (Mae) bent down to pick up the muddied sheet. "And bitch, if you touch my damn clothes again, I'm gonna—"

"You gonna what?" Bonnie wanted to fight Mae so bad. "If you think you gonna drive your nails into this family even more by waiting around for Daddy to die so you can take all his belongings, bitch please, I will kill you first!"

Mae stood there watching the foam spewing out from Bonnie's mouth. "Bonnie, you are going to run yourself into the grave worrying about me and my life if you don't watch out."

"You will be deep in your grave or living like a hobo on the street before I do, that's for sure, Mae. Why don't you take that bastard-ass baby everyone thinks is so damn cute, and that one-legged girl and get the hell out of our lives!" Bonnie threw down and trampled more sheets into the dirt.

I am pretty sure adults know that even though children can't understand language, they can certainly feel the energy and spirit that dwells in people, and God surely had his hand working in this situation from day one. I sat there on that table, looking like I was minding my own baby-business. The path He had for me was being carefully carved out, and as time went on and the buzz in the neighborhood died down, I continued to be the child that no one really said who the father was. Days turned into months and I grew up, enjoying the unconditional love of Jabo, Oda-Lee, Betty, and Candy, who never really grasped the understanding of me being her son. That was my world.

As the months turned into years, it became plainer and plainer that I was looking very much like...well, don't let me get too ahead of myself. There are more minds to be blown and more story to be told, and I am going to tell it.

chapter 25

Chickens Coming Home to Roost

"Look at that beautiful baby. Come to Anie, child. I'm taking you to the park today," Oda-Lee said. She packed a bag and took me to the car with her and Betty.

"Oda-Lee, don't be driving like a bat outta hell with my baby in the car!" Jabo yelled from the porch.

"I'm not driving crazy, Jabo, calm yo ass down!"

"Hi, Anie," Candy said from the other side of the porch.

"Hey, Candy, girl. How are you, baby?"

"Good," Candy said with a smile and that babylike voice she was known for. She continued to play with her dolls at Jabo's feet.

As I am writing these words, I realize how much more invisible Candy became after I arrived. I mean, the poor girl was already nearly non-existent, but when I arrived, she got even less time and attention, except for maybe from Jabo. She had to deal with a lot, and it is always good to remember that you never really know what someone has been through just by looking at them. Yet just by looking at that poor little girl, there had to have been some sad shit going on.

Thank the Lord for Anie and her sense of right and wrong... and humor.

Anie drove up to the McDonald's window. "I want two Big Macs, two small fries, two orange drinks, and a Happy Meal."

"You said small fries, right?" the girl repeated over the intercom.

"No, I said large."

"Okay, so two large fries, two Big Macs, and two orange drinks," the young lady said.

"Girl, I told you two Quarter Pounders, two small fries, and two Pepsis. I don't understand what the damn problem is with you not hearing what I want." Oda-Lee looked over at Betty and rolled her eyes. "Girl, you don't need to be workin' here if you don't know how to take a damn order." She stepped on the gas and drove the car around to the window. "Lord have mercy, look at this beautiful girl. She just as pretty as she can be." Anie laughed. "Yes, honey, I ordered two Big Macs, two small fries, two orange drinks, and a Happy Meal for the baby."

"Absolutely, ma'am, coming right up," the girl answered, so charmed by Oda-Lee that she couldn't fault the old lady for not getting her order right the first (or second) time.

Anie sang while we waited for the pretty girl to fill the order. Even as a baby, I smiled every time she sang. Anie had a terrible voice, but the love coming through every one of those horrible notes would tell me how dearly this woman loved me.

* * *

"Hey there, baby, how are you?" Bonnie pulled the phone cord all the way out on the front porch to see who was next door. "Hey, everybody, it's June Bug!" she said so loudly that everyone three blocks in either direction could hear her.

"June Bug?" Jabo wheeled himself out of the house and onto the porch. I'm not sure how the hell he got out of bed, to his chair, and then to the porch so quickly, but I'll just imagine he was waiting by the window. "Let me talk to him."

At that time there was no such thing as a cordless phone, so Bonnie took it upon herself to yell back and forth. "He said, 'Hey, Daddy.'"

"Tell that boy I love him, and I want to see him soon," Jabo yelled over to her, which was hard since the poor man was losing strength daily.

"He said to tell you he'll be coming home in a couple months, Daddy, and not to worry," Bonnie relayed.

"Tell him he's gotta hurry so he can see the new baby."

Suddenly someone yelled from across the street, "Damn, you two, shut the hell up!"

Kevin had been gone about two and a half years, and in that time Jabo had deteriorated so much he was hardly recognizable. Everyone was shocked at how long he actually did manage to hang on, considering he had diabetes *and* cancer, and there wasn't much anyone could really do about either. He was basically skin and bones by that point.

Mae was spending more and more time at "night service" while everyone else slept, and although things continued like that for a while, it was only a matter of time before it all went to hell. While planes and cars can go on cruise control, people can't, and that static never works for any period of time. Something will always give, one way or another.

One morning, shortly before the next hellfire hit the fan, I was playing next to Candy when Jabo looked at me and said, "Come here, boy." I tried to crawl over to him, but I was so fat I could hardly move.

I outstretched my arms and grumbled, "Dada, dada!"

"Did you hear that?" he said to no one in particular. "He said Daddy." The biggest tears welled up in his eyes and he broke down crying. "Boy, I love you so much. I'm not sure what that boy gonna do for you, probably nothing, but I'm gonna make sure you have everything you need and that you will be loved."

It was another promise Jabo made that he was not going to be able to keep.

chapter 26

Death of a Patriarch

It was a Sunday morning and Mae got up wanting some peace and quiet before having to get ready for church. (Isn't it funny how they never miss a Sunday but create hell all week? I guess that's what church is for, trying to get it right the next time.) After about an hour of bumping around in the kitchen, making coffee and getting things ready for breakfast, something whispered in her ear to go and check in on Jabo. She poured him a cup of coffee with two sugars (yeah, everyone stopped caring about that sugar thing once they knew it wouldn't help anyway) and almost dropped it when she walked into the room and saw Jabo sitting upright in bed, gazing at her with an eerie, blank stare.

"Jabo, are you okay?" she asked. He didn't respond. She set the cup down on the nightstand and sat next to him on the bed. "Jabo?" She laid her hand on his. It was cold. She checked to see if he was breathing. He was.

Candy came crawling into the room to hear what Mae was yelling about, but I was sound asleep, even though my crib was right by his bed.

"What's wrong, Momma?" Candy asked.

"I'mma call 911, something's wrong with—"

"No, babe, don't call 911. Gather the family," Jabo said. "I want to see everyone." He smiled slightly and closed his eyes. "Don't worry, babe. I'm all right. I just saw Jesus, and He told me that everything I have ever worried about is going to be just fine."

Tears welled up in Mae's eyes and she believed what Jabo said Jesus told him was true. "Okay, Jabo. I'll go and get everyone. Candy, you stay here with Daddy and the baby. I'll be right back."

Mae ran next door to Bonnie's and banged on the door. She came quickly, rollers in her hair and wearing a huge white house robe, knowing right away that something was wrong because Mae had never stepped foot over there once. "What's wrong with Daddy?" she asked in a panic, trying to put her glasses on properly.

"Come over now, he ain't got long," Mae said and went back down the stairs.

"I'll call Anie and—" Right at that moment Oda-Lee's big brown sedan pulled up with Oda-Lee and Betty getting out before it was even in park. Mae was at curb when the two ladies got out.

"How is Jabo doing? Child, something told me to swing by before I went to Sunday school. I knew he wasn't feeling well."

"Oda-Lee, God must have told you. He ain't doing good at all," Mae said and ushered everyone in.

They went into the bedroom and Bonnie appeared a few moments later.

"Well, damn, why is it I gotta be fixin' to meet Jesus to get y'all all together without biting each other's head off?" Jabo looked around at the women who had caused him so much pain in his life, but also so much joy.

"How you doing, brother?" Oda-Lee hugged him, fighting back her emotions. By the glazed look in his eyes, she could tell, sure as day, he wouldn't have much time left here in this world.

"I'm doin' like I been doin' all my life. Now listen carefully, okay? 'Cause I'm gonna run this down for y'all while I still got the strength.

Oda-Lee, you the last one left of our generation so I want you to look after this family as best as you can. All your life I have looked after you, and in your own way you have always looked after me. I'm honored to have been chosen by God to be your brother all these years."

"Lord, Jabo, you are something else." Tears rolled down Oda-Lee's face. She took out a tissue and wiped them away. "I am going to miss you more than you can imagine."

"Momma would be so proud of her daughter and the caring woman you have become. And Daddy would have said, 'Look at my little mutt.' Now stop your crying and give me a hug."

Oda-Lee reached over and hugged her brother's bony frame again, and when she did, I have been told that I woke up and started smiling, looking through the bars of my crib at the two most beloved people in my world.

Jabo looked over and saw me. "Most of all, Oda-Lee, you is my witness and I want to say this in front of everybody. I don't care what none of them do with anything else, I need you to take care of this boy because Kevin ain't gonna do shit for him, that's for sho."

Bonnie was about to open her mouth, but she knew better.

"Yes, Jabo, I will," Oda-Lee said through her sniffles.

"Mae, honey, you are my light and I love you more than you know. I understand that I'm older than you and that you probably wanted other things. We never even did much traveling like I said I wanted, but life is life, and I do know that you loved me as much as I loved you. I just want to remind you, though, that nothing is as sweet inside as it might look on the outside." He coughed a bit, then continued. "You're now free to be with whoever you want, so make sure you know what you're doing, and especially who you doing it with. These babies right here are depending on you."

"Yes, Jabo." Fighting back tears, Mae kissed him on the lips for what would surely be the last time.

"Bonnie," he said somewhat harshly.

"Daddy!" she screamed and moved Mae aside so she could get close.

He took her hand. "Yes, my little girl, I'm leaving now. Leaving means letting go, so I want you to do the same and let go of some of the things that you hold onto so tightly and start to forgive. I want you to forgive me for things you don't understand and for the things that you do. Forgive them too."

"I will, Daddy, I love you so much."

"I know you do, Bonnie, and even though you have shown this love for me in ways that have not always been best for everyone, I understand you and why you do it. But I need you to promise me you will take care of your family and do the right thing by Mae and these kids. Do you hear me?"

"Yes, Daddy, I hear you and I wouldn't dare go against your wishes." She kissed him on his cheek and stood aside for Betty to come forward.

"Betty, my sweet niece, please continue to take care of your momma. You are the shining star of Oda-Lee and Johnny. I love you, babe." She gave her uncle a hug.

As a side note, Johnny was a friend of Jabo's who was married and had an adopted daughter, and up until that very moment, no one had ever known who Betty's father was except Oda-Lee, who acted like he hadn't said anything.

"Candy, come here, angel. I'm yo daddy and don't you forget that, okay, babe? I will love you forever and always."

"I love you too, Daddy." Candy crawled up onto the bed with a little help from Mae.

"Now hand me that baby," Jabo said, and when Mae reached over to pick me up, he said, "No. I want Bonnie to get him for me."

Bonnie reluctantly picked me up out of my crib and moved to place me in Jabo's arms. "No. Hold the boy up so I can see his face." She held me up for all to see. "I'm looking at an angel right there, the one who, out of all of us, was chosen to do something great, something big in a world that sorely needs it." He coughed again. "This boy is going to be the light of us all, but until that day comes, Bonnie, I'm looking into his face and next to his, I see yours. The only time I have ever seen this exact picture was when you were holding up June Bug just like this. You promise me you will do the right thing. This is your grandson...and you know it."

Bonnie continued to hold me, uncomfortable as it was for her. She was unable to hold Jabo's emotional gaze and amazingly enough, unlike most human beings with half a heart, she was unable to muster any feelings of love for the innocent young life she was holding in her hands.

"Damon Carter," Jabo mused. "God said, 'In the beginning there was the light' and you will always be that light that was at the end for me. I know now that my legacy will go on."

The small group sat still, letting Jabo's words sink in and their tears fall. He reached out his arms for Bonnie to lay me in them and looked down at me with the deepest of love in his eyes. "We never had a middle name for you. It took all this time."

"Jabo, I was thinking, why don't we call him Damon Terrell?" Oda-Lee suggested. I guess naming me was a group effort.

"Terrell..." he chuckled softly. "I think I love that more than Damon. I want y'all to put that on his birth certificate. Damon Terrell Carter. How I..." He looked around the room one last time, took a breath, and smiled. His head slumped back, and his jaw went slack.

"*Daddy!*" Bonnie screamed.

Mae grabbed me and held me close, tears streaming down her face.

"He's gone," Oda-Lee said, shaking her head. "He's gone. My beautiful brother has gone to be with the King." She reached over and closed his eyes with the palm of her hand.

They all hugged each other and left the room one by one. Oda-Lee was the last one to go and before she walked out, she came back and kissed him on the forehead. "Goodnight, Alton Jabo Burder," she said for the last time and turned out the lights.

* * *

"Ashes to ashes, dust to dust..." The pastor sprinkled some dirt down into Jabo's grave. "As we dedicate this body back into the ground and this soul back into the hands of the Lord."

Everyone was quiet during the limo ride back to the church for the memorial dinner, but the air was so thick you'd have needed a sledgehammer to get through it.

Bonnie was, once again, that sledgehammer. "Since I got you all here in one place, I think it's the best time to talk about how we gon' split everything up."

Oda-Lee, Mae, and Betty looked at her in surprise.

"Yeah, well I think it's best you keep yo mouth shut for the time being, Bonnie," said Oda-Lee. "My brother ain't even cold yet. Give us a minute to grieve, for the sake of the Lord."

"No. I ain't gonna wait for nothing. Daddy wanted me to have both the houses and the other house that's down the street. That is a fact."

The limo driver looked back into the rearview mirror and couldn't believe his ears. In all his years, he ain't never hear no one talk about a will and testament and all the shit anyone owned on their way back from putting someone in the ground. Never. And he was old.

"What the hell are you on about, Bonnie? He told you to do right by us! I'm his wife, and we haven't even looked at the will yet!" Mae argued, but it was no use.

"There is no will," Bonnie said. "I know what he wants and what he would have wanted. What he said when he was dying was just sentimental bullshit." Bonnie said those words as softly as she could when she sensed the driver looking at her and while looking away from the three women staring at her in the face. "If nothing's written down on paper, then it's what's in my mind that's the truth. You can stay in the house until you find some other place to stay as long as it's within thirty days."

"Thirty days! What in the hell do you expect us to do?"

"What you always done. Find someone to get you out of the mess you got yo ass into."

Oda-Lee was burning up. "Bonnie, you should be ashamed of yourself talking like this after your father ain't even in the damn ground."

The conversation ended there because the limo was pulling up to the church.

Everyone filed out of the car with their attitudes but while Oda-Lee, Betty, and Bonnie marched into the church, Mae got into her car with me and Candy and drove off.

"Mae!" Oda-Lee yelled as Mae pulled away. She walked back over to the church and down into the basement where all the guests were milling about, waiting for the family to arrive. Oda-Lee got up to the head of the room and stood there for a moment while everyone got settled then said, "Today I put my only brother in the ground, and my sorrow is overshadowed only by the shame I feel at the hands of his daughter." She looked right at Bonnie, who appeared perfectly oblivious to the fact that Oda-Lee was talking about her. "Her father would not only be embarrassed by the selfishness she has shown in the last three days, but he would feel anger, hurt, and betrayal. I can't even stay and eat with her. Come on Betty, we're leaving."

Betty, who had already gone over to the line for food, put her plate down and followed her mother out of the church. This was officially the beginning of World War Three.

chapter 27

Moving Day

Exactly thirty days later at 5:30 a.m., there was a knock on the door. Mae, trying to keep her robe closed, opened the door to the sheriff with Bonnie standing behind him, her arms crossed over her massive bosom, with no bra on, lookin' like she just had puppies.

"Good morning, Missus Burder. Sorry to bother you so early in the morning." The sheriff glanced over at Bonnie for a brief second then continued with his script. "I'm Sheriff Johnson of the New York State Authorities and I'm here to serve you with your final eviction notice to vacate the premises of this residence by 5:00 p.m. today."

"Final? What are you talking about? I haven't...we didn't get any notices. I thought we were working this thing out, Bonnie," Mae pleaded, but it was no use.

"Bitch, get you and yo shit out of my house and take all of your bastard-ass children and that problem child with you," Bonnie said with an evil look.

"But...we don't even have anything lined up. We have no idea where we gonna live."

"Do I look like I care? You had plenty of time to get yo shit together."

"Actually, Missus Burder, there were a number of notices sent and left on the door. Maybe someone removed them?" the sheriff asked carefully. You could tell he was a nice man, simply doing his job, and feeling mighty sorry for this poor woman. He was pretty sure this Bonnie lady was moving the notices, but that wasn't his main concern right now. His job was making sure it wouldn't get so loud they'd wake the neighbors and keep it from getting uglier than it already was.

"I have not seen anything of the kind, officer, you have my word."

"Bitch, shut up and stop with the excuses. Get yo shit and get out of here *now*! You have until the end of the day to vacate. That means five o'clock. I know you wouldn't know what end of day is since you ain't neva had an honest job, 'cause hoin' don't count."

"Ma'am, would you please just let me handle this?" He turned his attention back to Mae. "I'm very sorry, ma'am, and I'm sure there's an explanation, but unfortunately, I can only go by what's written here." He handed her the documents.

"The end of the day," Bonnie said.

"Yes, the end of the day," the sheriff repeated in a kinder tone. "That is, unless you want us to investigate what happened to the documents...?" But Mae was done. She'd figure something out.

"Thank you, officer, but I think it's best we leave."

With that, Bonnie looked at the two of them as if she had been deeply betrayed and walked off the porch. "The locks will be changed at 5:01." She marched across the grass, onto her porch, and slammed the door behind her.

"Thank you for your kindness, officer. I don't want to cause any trouble, so I'll get moved out by the end of the day."

"I'm really sorry, Missus Burder. I'm sure there's more to this than meets the eye, but sadly, I have to follow the rules. I always liked Alton Burder. I am truly sorry for your loss." He tipped his hat and left the porch.

Mae closed the door and looked out the window as he drove away.

"What's wrong, baby, who was that?" came a sleepy voice from out of the back bedroom.

"It was that lyin' bitch from next door with the sheriff telling me I have to be out of the house by the end of the day."

"Then you're just gonna have to get out of here. Don't worry, I'll help you."

"How are you going to help me?" Mae said, turning around to face the man who was now holding his arms out to her. "You have a wife and eight children. This is all just going to be a mess."

"We've been getting by this long, babe, just a while longer and we will make it all happen the way that we want it to happen. I love you, Mae." He hugged her tight.

"I love you too, Charles."

* * *

"Momma, it's me."

"*Me?*" Granny said on her end of the phone. "*Hell, I have seventeen children, fifteen still living. Who the hell is 'me'?*"

"Mae, Momma," she sobbed. "I don't know what to do."

"*What's wrong?*"

"Bonnie had the police come and serve papers to me today and said I had to be out of the house by five p.m....with Candy and the baby."

"*What!? Good Lord, what is wrong with that woman? She's possessed by the devil and something else. I'm mighty glad I only met with Jabo, Oda-Lee, and Betty from over there. You know me, anything that gives me a problem I stay away from it. Now you just go on and get away from there once and for all, ya hear?*"

"Yes Momma, but where'm I gonna go?"

Granny hesitated, then said, "*You know I got that upstairs free right now but, Mae honey, I need somebody in there that's gonna pay rent.*"

"I know, Momma, you can trust me. I swear I'll have the rent paid every month."

"How you gonna swear to that? You ain't even got no job!"

"Bonnie don't know this, but Jabo left me a little money in the safe, so I can give that to you until I figure something out. Oh, and it won't be just me and the kids," Mae said, bracing herself for the tornado that was bound to come from the other end.

"Who else is going to live with you?" Granny asked skeptically.

A moment of silence. Then, "Charles."

"Charles Whitehead?" Granny said, almost dropping the phone.

"Yes, Charles Whitehead."

Granny took a long breath. *"Mae, you know I love you, child, but are you crazy? That man is married with eight kids to support, not to mention he's your dead husband's nephew or cousin or whatever he is. Everyone who ever introduced him always said one or the other. Mae, you swore up and down on a stack of bibles that you weren't messin' with that man."*

"Yes, Momma, I know, but I can't worry about any of that right now. All I know is I love him, he loves me, we wanna live together, and I gotta get my ass out of this house," Mae said through a crackly voice flooded with tears. "He has a good job, so I know he'll help me. Momma, please, you have to give me a chance."

After a moment Granny said, *"All right, girl, come on and bring yo stuff."*

By the skin of her teeth, Momma Mae was able to get the hell out of Jabo's house and set up shop at 109 Landon, right above her own mother, along with the married nephew of her dead husband who had died only thirty days before.

This is a prime example of making decisions based on your present situation.

* * *

We were just about settled into 109 Landon when, not even a week later, the phone rang at four o'clock in the morning, on the dot.

"Hello?" Momma (Mae) answered, half asleep.

"Get Charles's ass on this line and get it on here now!" It was Mary, Charles's wife.

In Mae's defense, Charles and Mary were an on again-off again kind of thing, and Mary was something we might in modern terms call bi-polar, to hear him tell it. However, knowing what I know now, she was woman who had been hurt by this man and couldn't let go. There is a fine line between scorned and bi-polar, so both can look very much like the other when the heart is involved. Knowing what I know now about Charles, I'm convinced he was too. Yet the fact remains that Momma and Charles were sneaking around for years behind everyone's back, so that probably had a lot to do with the craziness.

"Mary, Charles ain't here. I tell you that every time you call me, and you keep on calling," Momma said, which was a bold-faced lie, but it was only due to self-preservation since she knew how crazy Mary was.

"Damn you, Mae, I know he's over there." Abruptly, she calmed down and began speaking evenly. *"Look, Mae, I don't have no issues with you, but I do know that my husband is a no-good bastard, so you better let me talk to him."*

"Mary, I'm going back to bed, and I'm not even sure how you got my number but—"

"Never mind. Goodbye." She slammed the phone down right in Momma's ear.

"Charles, that woman you're married to is a psycho, you know that, don't you?"

"Yes, I know. Her elevator don't go all the way to the top," he joked.

"I'm serious, Charles, and you need to take this seriously too, or else she gonna do something none of us is gonna like."

"Yeah, yeah, I know, I know." He went into the bathroom to take a piss. When he came out, he got back into bed and took Mae in his arms. "I'll talk to her later when we up, okay, babe?"

"Thank you. That makes me feel a bit better."

They fell asleep in each other's arms.

Shortly thereafter there was a loud banging on the door that sounded like it might crunch any second under the pressure. Mae woke up first, her heart beating fast.

"Charles! Get yo ass down here or I will bust down this door!" Mary yelled on the other side.

"Call the police, Charles!" Mae said. "She gonna wake up the whole neighborhood if she hasn't already."

"Yeah, call the police. She crazy." Charles rolled onto his other side.

"Get up! Charles!" Mae urged, but it was no use, he was back to snoring.

Charles had a way of dismissing everything like it was nothing, which was probably a factor in the mess they were in today. Mae shook her head in exasperation and called the police, waiting impatiently until she heard the sirens, worried that Granny would wake up and be pissed at her for bringing that shit to her house.

The police confronted Mary on the front porch. "What is all the commotion, ma'am? We've had complaints from the neighbors. Do you live here?"

"Hell, no. My husband's in there and I'm fixin' to…" Mary didn't finish her sentence because she herself wasn't really sure what she was fixing to do.

The policeman took her gently by the arm and led her down the steps. "Ma'am, it's six in the morning. Maybe you can fix whatever it is later so you don't disrupt the entire street. Can we give you a ride home?"

"I'm gonna…gonna…" She looked at the police officer as if she had just woken from a trance. "What did you say?"

"I asked if we could give you a ride home," he said kindly.

"I got my own damn car." Mary shrugged the officer's hand off her arm and got into her beat-up old Ford.

The officers stood on the sidewalk until the car was out of sight then nodded to each other as if to say, "Donut time?"

Meanwhile, all that racket inside our apartment had woken me up and I started fussing, so Momma got out of bed to see to my needs.

"Charles," she said before leaving the room with me. "Charles?" but he was out like a light.

* * *

"Morning," Granny said. She was sitting on the front porch when Mae came out of the house.

"Good morning, Granny," Momma said sheepishly, sitting next to her mother.

Mae called her mother Granny like everybody else. I learned this was because all of the older generation sometimes called all their kids the only one name they could think of at the time, and somehow the kids always knew who they were talking about.

"I heard all of the fuss going on last night so I came to the window," Granny said with her bowl of cornbread and buttermilk she would so often be eating.

Momma stated to explain. "Yes, that was—"

"Girl, I know who that was, and I knew this was going to happen. I tried giving y'all the benefit of the doubt, but I ain't gonna have all that mess going on over here, ya hear me, sis?" Granny said.

"Granny, I didn't think anything like that would happen. I—"

"Well, girl-child, I don't know what you *thought* was going to happen, but that ain't rarely the case. You know that woman is crazy, and what you two have done is just making her crazier."

"Yes, Granny, I know. I guess I just didn't know *how* crazy."

"You better fix this mess quick or I'm sorry, but you gonna have to go somewhere else." Granny never looked up from her bowl.

"Granny, I know, but I got the children and I—"

"I said you. The children ain't gotta go nowhere." Momma looked at Granny and for a moment didn't know what to do. Then Granny looked up and they both started laughing.

"Granny, I know I'm in a bit of a mess right now, but it's going to be okay. I'm thinking of going to school and getting myself a degree in nursing."

"That is a great idea. I think you should! In the meantime, you just gotta be careful, you hear me, sis?"

"You hear me, sis?" was one of Granny's favorite lines. She would say it to everyone; her children, her sisters, her brothers, their kids, her pastor, the mailman, they shopkeeper on the corner, it didn't matter. If she was saying something, she would say that to seal the deal. Another favorite was her answer to other people saying something like, "Take care," she would always answer with, "oka dake." Not "okey dokey," not "okey doke," but "oka dake." The only person that made any sense to was her...but this was my Granny.

* * *

The weeks went by and we finally settled into some kind of normalcy. Charles took care of the Mary problem by promising to give her enough money to take care of the bills and would go off to work and do what he had to do. Momma Mae started nursing classes and eventually became a home care aide. That meant me and Candy were spending a lot of time alone together at the house, either sitting on the porch with Granny or laughing and playing with each other. We were more like brother and sister than mother and son.

"Happy birthday day, Terrell," Candy said so lovingly to me the morning of my fourth birthday. She would always sound like a baby herself, with that high pitched voice and crazy, mixed up grammar. Because of all the things she'd had to endure already, everybody babied her, and I think after a while she simply wasn't challenged to grow mentally or emotionally. The most important thing was that she was loved, and even that was hard to come by. "Let's go out to the big room," she said, which was the living room, but that's what she liked to call it.

I jumped out of bed and ran out of the room. Today was a special birthday because it was a Saturday, and that meant that Momma and Daddy (Charles, but I knew him as Daddy) would be home.

Me and Candy went out to the big room and there was a wonderful cake ready for me. Momma, Daddy, and Granny were sitting around the table, drinking coffee and having some laughs.

"Come here, boy," Granny said with her arms outstretched. She tried to lift me up, grunting and fussing. "Damn, child, you getting too big for me to put on my lap!"

Someone lit the candles and they sang the "Happy Birthday" song. I blew out the candles, and just as I was about to get my first piece of cake, the doorbell rang.

"I'll get it." Candy hobbled down the stairs to open the door. I knew the next voice anywhere.

"Hey, Candy, how you doing, girl? Where is my baby?" Anie said. "I know you didn't think I was going to let this day go by without coming over here and giving my baby a kiss and his birthday gift."

"Anie!" I jumped off my chair and ran over to hug her as she came up the stairs. I loved it when she came over. In fact, I kind of looked at her like she was the Fairy Godmother of my life, being the one who always showed me just how much she loved and cared for me, especially from my father's side of the family.

"Open ya gift, baby." She handed it to me.

"Can I eat some cake first?" I asked in all seriousness, and everyone laughed. I don't know when it happened, maybe I was just born with it, but my love for cakes and sweets started somewhere, and I am in no doubt that it started right from the minute I was born. Jabo had it too, if you'll recall, and it ended up being the death of him.

"Lord, this boy. He always ate only the sweet Gerber and never the peas and carrots," Momma said with a smile.

"Yes, baby, go ahead. Have your cake and eat it too."

I bit off a hunk of cake, then opened the package. Inside was my first suit. I was so happy, and I remember that day just like it was yesterday.

"You gonna always look good and clean 'cause now you old enough I'm gonna take you to church with me sometimes when Mae don't take you with her. Is that okay?" Anie asked no one in particular.

"Yes, of course, Oda-Lee," Mae answered. There was no way she was gonna tell Anie no, glad that Anie had gotten over the thing with her and Charles. Anie was a good soul and knew how to let people live, even after she gave you a piece of her mind.

"I love you, Anie." I gave her a big hug. This woman was my angel and I truly did enjoy those early years. It was a short time of happiness for us all.

chapter 28

The Settling of Affairs

"Hello, Missus Burder, please come in and have a seat,"

"Thank you, Mister Johnson," Mae said to the lawyer who had always handled Jabo's affairs.

"I called you in today regarding your late husband's estate. Mister Burder had fifty-three thousand dollars in savings, five thousand in his checking account, three homes, one car, and a retirement pension," Mr. Johnson read off from a piece of paper. "You are legally his wife and would normally have power of attorney over all of this, but..."

"But what?" Mae said, looking like she knew what was coming but didn't want to admit it.

"It seems there was a document signed by your husband and his daughter two days before he passed that transferred all of his assets over to her, stating you were not entitled to anything that belonged to her." He looked up briefly at Mae, knowing this would be a huge blow to her, but continued, hoping that what he was going to say next might cheer her up, at least a little. "The only thing it didn't mention was the continuation of his pension."

"What the hell are you talking about? He would never have signed anything like that! He told his daughter straight up to take care of us—on his deathbed!"

"I am afraid I wasn't there, so I cannot say if that was the case. But it states clearly here in black and white. I can have my secretary make a copy of it for your records if you like," he offered a bit helplessly.

"That bitch," Mae said under her breath.

"The only thing to discuss now would be the pension. As per the document, you are not entitled to any of his assets or anything that belonged to him," he continued carefully. "May I suggest we transfer the pension to your daughter Lela? The money would be available to her for the rest of her natural life, and I am sure it would come in very handy seeing as she is a cripple."

"How the hell you know that? I'm betting you had more than a few conversations with Missus Montinez [Bonnie's last name since she'd been married to the Puerto Rican gentleman] since you ain't never met my Candy. And anyway, she's 'special' not fuckin' crippled!" With that, Mae stormed out of Mr. Johnson's office and headed out to the parking lot to her car.

I can't imagine what Momma must have been feeling, having been betrayed by both Bonnie *and* Jabo. I'm sure she didn't think it was karma for sleeping with Charles all them years. I guess we never do think that way when it's something we did. Funny how we tend to forget our trespasses when someone trespasses against us. Another hard blow in a life filled with one after the other.

When Mae arrived at her car, she broke down in tears trying to find the key, screaming in frustration and letting out a cry that would have woken the devil. She was so tired of fighting all the time. When she got into the car, she let her head fall against the steering wheel.

* * *

Momma put me in the tub with my toys and began working on a quilt out in the living room. This activity gave her some peace and let her think of something else other than her troubles for a while.

"I can't hear you singing!" she called out. This was truly the beginning of "The Voice" for me, and although now I realize it might have been a way for her to save me from having to hear her and Charles arguing, it was how it all started.

"I'm singing, Momma! La, la, la, la...hear me?" I said loudly from the tub.

"Charles," Mae started in while he sat reading the newspaper, "you won't believe what that bitch is doing."

"What bitch, Mae?" he said with his nose still in the paper.

"Bonnie!"

"Oh, yeah, that bitch." Charles mumbled.

"She's taking everything. The houses, the money, everything." Mae burst into tears, even though she'd promised herself she wouldn't.

"Come on, babe, you don't need that shit anyway, we good." He looked up over the paper at her, then went back to reading the sports page. Charles was one of the most unemotional people I know. "Everything's gonna be fine, Mae. Let's just move on with our lives."

chapter 25

Living

Settling into a normal routine was an understatement, and for the first time ever, there was some kind of a structure to our family, a family that was very private. So private that the neighbors had no idea what the truth was. Like most families, I guess. Sometimes all peachy on the outside, but inside there's a pit rotting the rest of the nice, ripe fruit.

Candy was turning seventeen and about to graduate high school. We thought. While Momma was preparing for the big day, she received a call from the secretary at McKinley High School. After exchanging pleasantries, and correcting the lady for calling her Mrs. Carter instead of Mrs. Burder, the blow came.

"I'm calling to confirm with you what we are sure you already know, but your daughter Lela won't be graduating with her class due to poor attendance and low grades. Let me add that although we do sympathize with her condition, we are still unable to allow her to graduate."

They had a different situation for her back then, it wasn't like regular school, but a program for special needs students. She wasn't even going to get through that!

"Wait one minute here, I'm not sure what you're saying. My daughter should have near-perfect attendance. I know because I take her to school every day myself."

"Ma'am, that can't be right, since the school records tell me that she's missed over one hundred days of classes, many of which you yourself called in, telling us about the car accident and her near-death experience. Poor thing...."

"Near-death experience?" Mae repeated in disbelief. "I'll call you back." She slammed the phone down so hard it fell off the wall. "Candy!" she screamed at the top of her lungs. "Get your ass in here right this minute!"

Candy made her way into the kitchen doorway looking down at her one shoe, knowing what would be coming. I was standing right next to her because I wanted to know what Momma was so irate about.

"What the hell is this about you not going to school?"

"Momma, I—"

"*I*, shit. Come on over here, 'cause I'm gonna give you a near-death experience right now." Mae reached over and grabbed the closest thing she could find, which happened to be a wooden African spoon that was hanging on the wall for decoration, and started chasing Candy around the room to beat the hell out of her.

"Momma, stop! You hurting me!"

"I hope to hell I am!" Mae shouted, chasing Candy around the kitchen.

Watching the two of them reminded me of a baby buffalo running from a lion. Charles walked in casually. "What's going on in here?"

Mae stopped her walloping and looked over at Charles. "I have been dropping this girl off at school and she been goin' in the front door and walkin' right out the back."

"Candy, is that what you been doing? If so, you do indeed need an ass-whippin'." That was all he said before he retreated back to his den.

As for me, I stood there not knowing if I should laugh or cry. On the one hand it was a pretty hilarious scene and I couldn't help but burst into laughter, pointing at Candy, which made her cry even louder. On the other, it got me in a bunch of hot water. In fact, my punishment for laughing at my mother was to happen the very next morning.

* * *

"Mae, tell Bookie [the nickname Granny said she gave me, but at least three people swear they were the one to name me this, so I'm not sure where it came from] to get down here and help me!" Granny screamed up the back steps at six in the morning. To her, half the day was already gone.

Granny was always doing projects around the house that she would start, which Uncle Neil, one of her sons, would have to come and do all over again. I came downstairs, sleep still in my eyes, trying to figure out what an eight-year-old boy and an eighty-year-old woman could do around the house at six o'clock that was worth anything, except trying to teach me a lesson. No, I wouldn't be laughing now, that was for sure.

Granny was all wrapped up in the old, raggedy clothes she didn't mind getting dirty. "Bookie, I wanna paint the trim on this house as high up as we can reach, then Neil will come over here and finish the rest."

I was almost sure this would mean that our house would be two-tone for about nine months, and all the neighbors would be all pissed off again for having to look at yet another unfinished project.

"What color we going to paint it, Granny?"

"Mold," she said confidently.

"Mold?" I asked, trying not to laugh.

I looked down into the can and saw that sure as hell it wasn't no green-blue color of mold but mauve. I have to say I was relieved she'd only misspoken, but still a bit disappointed that our house was pretty much gonna be pink. Maybe Granny knew a thing or two about me already, making me help paint the house pink.

She had leaned the oldest ladder from the wreckage of a garage in the yard, the roof having fallen in the winter before from a heavy blizzard, up against the house. Uncle Neil was waiting "until the weather breaks," but since it was almost June, it looked like we would be waiting for him to finish the paint job for quite some time.

"Lord have mercy, this ladder is too high for us to be climbing on," Granny said with concern for me. I could stand there and reach the same height, so I'm not sure what she was talking about. "Well, it don't matter none since it's nice out and we can take our time."

I soon realized that Momma's "punishment" was a favor to Granny since she loved being out there with me, and it was then that we really started what was to be the bond I needed, the one I'd had with Anie. One thing about Granny, she had a way of telling it like it was...even when it wasn't.

chapter 30

The Open Door

"I want to welcome all of you to the Open Door Missionary Baptist Church," Reverend C.D. Bowman said with his booming voice to the congregation. "Wait one minute, who is that that we have sitting in the back, right over there? Do we have visitors? I would like to extend a very warm welcome to our white friends. White friends, would you please stand up?"

"Lord have mercy, Reverend Bowman, what in heaven's name is wrong with you?" Anie said under her breath in his direction, which was usually loud enough for everyone to hear it. "Those people know they white, they don't need you to point that out to them! Hell, we can see it too." She was completely disgusted.

Open Door was the church that Anie belonged to, and Betty would come along with her occasionally. But if there was something that could go wrong in a church, this was the place it would happen. The church was filled with a bunch of eighty-five-year-olds...and me.

"Well, I am the pastor here and I just want to say to these folks, you are welcome, and if you are welcome once, you are welcome twice, and you are welcome in the name of Jesus Christ. Terrell, would you please come up here and sing a few lines from 'Angels Keep Watching over Me'?"

While I didn't appreciate it then, now I see that Reverend Bowman was the first person who really pushed me to sing openly at churches, and because they had about five members at the time, I could practice all the songs and hymns I wanted without feeling too much like a fool. They did have a number of musicians, but the best one at the time was Ron.

Ron was about thirty-five years old with greasy, slicked-back hair, only gelled in the front, and his eyes were always bloodshot red. He smelled like a bottle of any kind of cheap brown liquor coupled with a peppermint. Yet Ron had a way of making that organ scream.

Reverend Bowman hated Ron because it was common knowledge that he was gay. This was before openness and liberation, before the rainbow meant something other than leprechauns and gold. Basically, Ron was an outcast and a threat to all the men, but the women loved him. He fired up the organ and I started wailing. Oda-Lee sat in the third row, stage right, with the happiest face, smiling and proud that I was her great-nephew.

After I finished the song and our "white friends" quietly tiptoed out, Reverend Bowman preached and we were ready to go home. The assistant pastor, Reverend Gar Sr., had a wife, a daughter, and a mentally challenged son. Back then we just called him retarded, which is rude, I know, but that was then. He wasn't really retarded, it was just that something didn't look or feel right with him.

After the service, Anie and I were talking to Reverend Bowman when Mrs. Gar came up to us, smiling sweetly.

"Hello, Sister Clay," Mrs. Gar said to Oda-Lee.

Oda-Lee smiled politely. "Hello there, Sister Gar."

"I just wanted to say that I loved Terrell's singing this morning. He reminds me so much of my Junior when he sings."

If you haven't noticed by now, Oda-Lee Clay was never one for keeping her mouth shut, and after she scoffed, she said, "You have got to be kidding me, girl. Terrell can sang, but Junior? That boy can't hardly talk!"

Betty magically appeared, pushing Reverend Bowman and Mrs. Bowman aside, and took her mother by the arm. "Momma, I think they need you in the shuttle van for the first load." She pulled me and Anie out the front door of the church. "Momma, get in that van. Hell, you can't say stuff like that!"

"Girl, she knew when she said that to me, she was being uppity."

"So let her have it once in a while, Momma."

"Ain't nobody gonna talk shit about my babe," she said, looking down at me.

I looked up at her and grinned. She always had a way of making me do that, even if it was sometimes a bit uncomfortable for others.

chapter 31

Babies Having Babies

Anie dropped me off at the house after church, but I bet if she'd heard what I heard when I walked in, she'd have turned right around with me in the car. Instead, we said our goodbyes and I ran upstairs, then straight to my room when I heard the firing range that was going on in the living room. I wasn't sure what was happening, but Momma and Charles were at it again, this time with an added character to the drama being played out. Candy was in the corner crying. I knew I had to go and check this out so I went to where I couldn't be seen, and in my Sunday church suit, I crouched down in the corner to listen.

When some black folks argue, it's hard to figure out what's going on, who's right and who's wrong, because most of the time everybody's yelling all at the same time. But this part I could hear:

"You just gonna have baby after baby, is that right?" Charles said, louder than I'd ever heard him talk.

"What the hell you talking about, Charles? Shit, you the one who done had baby after baby. You got eight of 'em!" Mae said in defense of her daughter, and of course she was right.

"That shit ain't the same and you know it, Mae," Charles countered and yeah, he was right too.

Candy got up her courage and said through her tears, "Momma, I'm sorry, I...I don't know how it happened."

"You don't know how it happened? I'll tell you what happened, you been having sex, that's how it happened, but this time you knew what the hell was going on." Momma broke out in tears. "The first time it wasn't your fault, but this time, I don't know, child...."

I knew what sex was even though they didn't think I did, but that wasn't what bothered me. It was the fact that Momma said the word *fault*. I went into my room and everything else faded into the background, all the noise and yelling and arguing. Confused and not knowing how to take what I'd just heard...it was the first time I realized I was actually some kind of mistake. I will never forget that pain I felt in my heart. What Momma said played over and over again in my head like a broken record. Up until then I had always thought I was special, that there was something extraordinary about me, but in that moment all I felt like was a mistake. Someone's *fault*. The last thing I felt in that moment was special.

Candy came in crying and slammed the door behind her, then jumped onto my bed, sobbing into the pillow. I had no idea what to do. I wanted to say everything would be okay, but how was a young kid like me supposed to know if anything would ever be okay for certain? With the way that things had been since the beginning, nothing had ever played all right. I guess it was just what people said. Our family never said "I love you" to each other, and even though I felt great love for her at that moment, I couldn't say it. It just wasn't something we did. It was something Anie and I did, but that was it. So I did what my nature told me to do. I rubbed her head and said, "It's going to be okay, Candy."

"Leave me alone!" she yelled.

Well, hell, I sure misjudged that one. I sat there watching her go through it, thinking of nothing but the fact that she was about to have another baby. One that was planned and special. Not like me.

* * *

Like everything in our family, the bickering and hollering soon died, the shit someone had stirred up would settle like dust, and life would go on until the next shitstorm kicked up. Which was just about to happen. I was gonna get a new playmate whose name was Dimples.

"Charles, what the hell do you mean she's on her way?" Momma yelled.

"Look, Mae, I wanted to tell you about this sooner, but I just couldn't find the time," Daddy said in the baritone voice he always used.

"Girl, what is going on in here?" Aunt-Sister said as she came upstairs from Granny's to see what all the fuss was about. Aunt-Sister was Momma's older sister who looked identical to Granny and actually looked more like she could be Granny's sister than her daughter, which was why Mae called her Aunt-Sister. She was known for saying all the things everyone else was thinking, but with a different spin than even Anie. Now that I think of it, they all were. I know where I get it from.

"Aunt-Sister, Charles has a damn daughter the same age as Bookie from some bitch from Cleveland he ain't said nothing about!" Momma shouted.

"Lord have mercy, Charles, you ought to be shamed," Aunt-Sister said.

The doorbell rang and a pretty lady came in very quietly and said hello to everyone. "Hi, I'm Sherri, it's nice to meet you," she said to Momma as sweet as could be, stretching out her hand.

"Sherri, girl, how are you doing, honey?" Momma said, even though she had just called the woman all kinds of bitches.

Sherri was a beautiful woman Charles had met when she was in Buffalo for her grandmother's funeral several years before. Everyone assumed they became more than friends—especially her husband. Yes, she was married when they began their affair but it, and her marriage, ended when the man showed up at Charles's job threatening him with a gun. Now it looked like Sherri had a new husband and he didn't want no kids running around the house, so Sherri decided she only had one option: Charles and his new lady. Any problems Momma had with any of that all went flying out the door when Momma saw her. It couldn't be denied that Sherri was a nice person and in fact, it was totally understandable why Charles would go for such a bombshell.

"We was fine until *you* got here," Aunt-Sister said under her breath and Momma stepped on her toe.

"I'm wonderful. Thank y'all for taking Dimples, I—"

"We don't need to know the whole story 'bout why you leaving that child," Aunt-Sister said, "but she gonna be fine." Momma stepped on her toe again.

"Hey, Sherri, put Dimples's bag over here," Charles said.

I started looking around and wondering where this "Dimples" was. That was when a little girl with the biggest, most beautiful dimples you ever wanted to see stepped out from behind Sherri's legs. She was the most adorable thing and also a bit shy.

"Hi, y'all," she said in a quiet voice.

Through all the cuteness there was one thing that really stuck out about her, and that was her hair. This girl's hair looked like a homeless man's hair. Like a sheep that hadn't been taken care of in years. We looked at each other and she walked right over to me and gave me a hug, then we both laughed. It was from that moment that the magic happened and she became my sister, the closest family member to me, the one that understood everything from my point of view and was always there dealing with it with me. I was so happy. I knew right then that I had a new partner in crime. I picked up her bag and we started off to the spare room when Charles said, "Ain't you gonna say goodbye to your Momma, Dimples?"

"Oh! I'm sorry, Momma! I'll see you later." She ran back over to her and hugged her mother, then the two of us went into Dimples's new room.

"You can have this bed," I said and set down her bag. Candy had vacated the room some time before, and come to think of it, I don't know where Candy lived most of the time.

"Where are you from?" I asked as we sat on the edge of the bed.

"From Cleveland."

I didn't have a clue where that was, and to be honest, I didn't really care. I was just so happy to have someone here that was my age who I could have fun with, even if it was a girl.

"Terrell! Come out here and get ready for bed!" Momma yelled from the living room after Sherri and Aunt-Sister had taken their leave.

"Have a good night and I'll see you the morning." I hugged her and left her alone in the room to her own thoughts. I danced into mine, knowing there was going to be a new, sweet energy in the house named Dimples.

chapter 32

The Neighbors

"Ty-Rell," Mrs. Mary said from her porch.

"Yeah?" I yelled back from the yard and ran out to see what she wanted. Before I could get all the way up to the porch, there she stood, a lady with the purple, caked-on makeup that damn near illuminated the entire neighborhood, but was also dull and green at the same time. She looked exactly like whatever visions of an alien you have in your mind right now or have ever imagined in your entire life. Or the title to the movie *Something Wicked This Way Comes*, or Evelin from *The Wiz*. Mrs. Mary fit each and every one of them. However, she was sweet as could be...sometimes.

"Can you go to the store and get me a pack of Mores? Menthol, darling, the ones in the green pack."

"Yes, Mary," I said, and off to the store I went, singing and humming to myself. I knew she was gonna ask me to get Mores menthols because that's all Mrs. Mary smoked, but she said it every time, as if I forgot. She wasn't condescending, just one of those black people that lived in the hood and thought she was better than the others, even though her house was right next door to ours. I mean, all she had to say was, "Get me a pack of cigarettes," and I would've known what she wanted, and she knew I knew, because she asked me nearly every damn day. But I didn't mind routine. Actually, now that I think of it, I hated going to get her damn cigarettes because every time I reached the corner, a very familiar face appeared from around it.

"Well, well, well, would you look at this bitch," the long, lanky boy said. Lizard was known for constantly terrorizing the kids in the neighborhood and chasing us home. Lizard looked like a black iguana that would bite you right in the face and needless to say, I was terrified of him. Lizard and I played doctor once or twice behind the store, but I'll get into that another time. I took off running towards the store to get them damn Mores, running so fast there were shoe prints on the back of my shorts. If I had nightmares, it would be about Lizard catching me one day and killing me, unless he played a few rounds of pocket pool, but that's also another story because now I was just worried about him eating the meat off my bones. What I didn't know was that behind my back he was laughing his black iguana ass off.

Lizard liked his reputation as the neighborhood bully, but no one ever reported him doing anything to anyone, only scaring the living shit out of them and stealing from the corner shop. All the same, no one could stand the guy, and he was simply known for being an idiot and a bully. When I think about him now, I wonder what kind of messed up family life he had because I know he must have had some momma and daddy iguanas and some iguana siblings.

I reached the store and burst the door open.

"Hey! What you do?" Habib, the owner of the corner store who everyone called Nick, said. "Hey guy, don't slam door!"

I don't know how he got a name like Nick since he was Arabian, which is what we thought at the time, but that's just like the pot calling the kettle black because have any of these nicknames in my family made any sense to you? I didn't think so.

"I'm sorry, Nick, Lizard's chasing me!" I said, out of breath.

"Dumb ass Snap. He steal from store all time," Nick said in broken English, even though he'd been living in Buffalo forever. I loved Nick and he was a great dude. Lizard walked up to the front window of the store all cool as could be with his hands in his pockets like he was about to browse through a museum. Nick went to the door, opened it and said, "Get out of here, get from front of my store, dumb boy."

"Shut yo ass up before I shit on these steps," was Lizard's dumb-ass, but admittedly funny reply.

"You no leave, I call the cop like last time!"

Lizard flipped him off and ran around the other corner.

"You can go now the way you came from home, Terrell."

"Thank you! Oh! I need some—"

"Mores menthols. I know, they for Miss Mary. Here, already in the bag," Nick said, rolling both *R*s in my name as hard as he could, spit flying all over the counters, change, and the bag with that pack of Mores menthol cigarettes.

I snatched the bag and ran out the door.

"You say Miss Mary she need to pay her bill!" Nick yelled after me.

I ran home, looking over my shoulder for those black scales coming out of every garage and driveway.

"Ty-Rell, why thank you so much, I appreciate you for going for me," Mrs. Mary said, handing me a plate full of greens and a wet dollar bill out of her bra that looked like she had had it since she was a little girl. I was so grateful for the money though. I ran into the house and sat at the kitchen table, then unwrapped the greens.

Dimples walked in and busted out laughing. "She gave you *that shit* for going to the store? That's exactly why I stopped going for her ass. Her and that Lizard asshole too."

After thinking about it, I was a bit ashamed, especially when I tasted them. They tasted exactly like that dollar bill she gave me. I looked at Dimples and, as always, we busted out laughing as we so often did.

"Throw that shit in the garbage," she said, as she leaned over, then did it herself.

God, I love that girl.

chapter 33

The Pimp Returns

"Hey, anybody in here? Momma? It's me, Gerry!"

"Gerry here, y'all!" Candy said, crawling to the front of the house.

"What you doin' here?" Momma asked skeptically.

"I thought I'd surprise you," he said to Momma. If you'll recall, Gerry was Momma's eldest son and had been away in the Army when my story began. The two of them were really close in age because she was only fourteen when she had him, so he was more like her brother. He had been gone as long as anyone could remember, so when he showed up, there had to be a reason for it.

Gerry was a pimp in NYC, had hos and tons of money, and looked like Superfly. "Well, now, who is this young lady ya got with you?" Momma asked, knowing full well this "young lady" was some ho of his. Next to Gerry was some pale, skinny-ass white girl half his age, standing there looking like she had just had a line of coke, threw up, and was ready for her hourly laxative pill. Pretty face though.

"I'm Shirley," the young lady said while grinding her teeth like an old mule chewing hay, except her mouth was empty.

"Hello, Shirley girl," Momma said, and sat down on the couch to watch how the next act was gonna unfold.

"Momma, this is for you," Gerry said, handing her a large garbage bag.

"What the hell? I don't need more garbage!" Momma said with a smile, then she opened the bag and saw a mountain of cash. It was all one-dollar bills, but it looked like a million to us. "Oh my God! You are my favorite son!" Now that he was giving her money, he was Momma's favorite.

Gerry was tall, fine as hell, and the kind of man that every woman wanted to and did have sex with.

Momma sat right there in the kitchen and counted every dollar. "Nine hundred and ninety-nine, one thousand," she said, slamming the bills down onto the table.

"Do you have any syrup and bread?" Shirley asked meekly.

"You don't want no meat?" Momma asked back, looking at the girl over the top of her glasses.

"Bread and syrup, that's all," the poor girl told Momma.

I remember feeling sorry for this girl. I thought she must have run away from her family and fallen into Gerry's evil-ass hands.

"Over there on top of the refrigerator is the bread, and the syrup is on the counter."

The girl walked over, got her a plate, and made the useless meal. I couldn't help but feel sorry for her. Even at my young age, I knew this was someone's daughter and she wasn't doing too well. Then I looked over at Gerry, not knowing how to place him. He clearly had no respect for women, or anyone for that matter, he cursed like a sailor, and was rude and obnoxious, yet I couldn't help wanting to have his presence. I wanted to be noticed and respected the way he was respected. He was a stunning man with an amazing body and an even better smile and knew how to get whatever he wanted in life. A true alpha male who would let nothing stand in his way.

Funny thing is, I'm looking at all these fucked-up men in my family and I realize I've taken on so many of their traits. The way Gerry walks into a room larger than life, Willie's meekness but sense of how to treat people, and Charles's moodiness and ability to say some of the meanest shit to people. The list goes on.

chapter 34

Bingo, Part Two

"Okay, okay, I'm coming, just let me get my stuff together!" Momma yelled down to Granny, who would never come up the stairs.

They were going to bingo. The funny thing was, they would walk about half a mile down to the bingo place, but Granny thought there were too many steps to climb up to our apartment.

"Mae, I'm not going to be late. I'm gone." Granny stepped off into the street and started the walk towards Jefferson Avenue at a turtle's pace.

Miss Aletha came running up and screamed, "W-w-wait for m-m-me, Granny!"

You remember Miss Aletha, don't you? If not, go back to chapter twenty and refresh your memory. (Hint: Grape Ape)

"You better come on, Letha!" Granny yelled back at her.

"Terrell, you and Dimples be good, hear? I'll be back in about two hours."

"Yes, Momma," we both said as she rushed out the door to catch Granny and Miss Aletha. Dimples never called Momma anything but Momma. From the minute she stepped into our house, she was part of the family.

"Let's play Pac-Man!" I said, all excited.

"Oh, yes, I know I'm going to beat you," Dimples said, and we weren't five minutes into the game when the front door opened, and the presence of evil entered the room.

"What the hell y'all bad asses doing?" Gerry asked, coming back inside by himself. I'm not sure where his skinny white girl was, and we really didn't care. More than likely she was out making them more money. "Where'd Momma go?" he asked, but we were so into the game neither one of us really answered.

"Terrell, you mothafucka. Didn't you hear what I said?"

"Bingo," I answered, still going hard on the controller.

"Oh my God, I swear I'm about to get you!" Dimples laughed until there was that familiar sound. *Womp, Womp, Womp.*

"Oh yeah! I knew I'd get you! I won! I won!" I was jumping up and down when Gerry came up to us and spoke to Dimples, who was still trying to get over the fact I whipped her ass.

"Dimples, would you come in here and help me with something I bought for Shirley?" Gerry asked as smoothly as only he could.

I decided to start a solo game and to keep the momentum going. "Come on, ghost, don't..." I continued talking to the game when I realized about a half hour had gone by and Dimples hadn't come back yet. I decided to go and see where the hell she was, and I went in the direction Gerry had taken her. I opened her bedroom door slightly to see if she was in there. For some reason, I had totally forgotten Gerry was even there.

"Dimples, are you...?" I stopped in my tracks when I saw Gerry, completely naked, on top of Dimples, who clearly looked like she didn't know what the hell was going on.

"What are y'all doing?" I asked.

"What does it look like, punk?" Gerry continued to force himself inside Dimples.

We were just kids at the time and Gerry was known for making even the largest of men look small.

"Gerry, you're hurting me," Dimples complained, and I could see she was crying.

"It's supposed to hurt, that's okay," he assured her.

I didn't know what to do. I was in a bit of a shock...but curious. Even though I had never done anything sexual at the time, I knew exactly what sex was. And even though I knew what was going down in this room was wrong, Gerry was an adult, and my hero in so many ways, so I couldn't say anything. I stood there in shock as he continued trying to push himself inside her. Dimples looked over at me, but I was cemented to the floor and couldn't move. If only I had known that this would be the beginning of so many problems for both Dimples and me.

chapter 35

The Letter

"There's a letter from the school board," Momma said when she came home, waving a piece of paper in front of my face. She opened it then read aloud: "Greetings from the Buffalo District School Board. We would like to offer your child Damon Terrell Carter a chance to attend school number forty-five on the west side of Buffalo. This is an attempt to introduce students to other parts of the city. We need to know before August twenty-first to ensure transportation and enrollment." Momma looked up at me. "I think this is good for you, Terrell, what you think?"

"You mean I would be catching a bus instead of going to school here in the fall?" My immediate thought was that I wouldn't be going to school with Lizard anymore, so I didn't give a damn if the school was in Florida. "Yeah, I want to go." I thought it would be fun and I'd get a chance to meet other people and different races and cultures, which had always intrigued me.

"I'll make the call in the morning," Momma said. "You and Dimples get ready, I gotta go and take Granny to get her hair done."

Dimples came into the room looking for her shoes. "I can't find my jellies."

"Girl, the shoe is right there under the couch. If it had been a snake it would have bit you," Momma said. "And what in the devil is wrong with your hair?" Momma tried her best to put her fingers through it. "It looks like man's hair, Dimples."

"What, you just noticing that now?" I said and we all started to laugh.

"Well, hell, we gonna get y'all's done too!" said Momma.

* * *

Later that evening we walked back into the house to find Daddy sitting at the kitchen table eating some chicken he had cooked that was burnt on the outside and raw inside. We all had gotten our hair done and now had what they called Jheri Curls. Jheri Curls were a way your hair would look curly and silky as long as you put activator and moisturizer on it every day. The downside was that you couldn't wash your hair but once a month, and this would fuck up all your pillows and erode the paint off the headboard of your bed. No one ever stopped to think what it was doing to our insides.

"What the hell y'all got in yo head? All that damn grease." Daddy shook his head and wiped chicken grease off his chin. "Bookie, what the hell you doin' with that shit?" he asked me. "That shit's for girls. You suppose to go to the barbershop with me! What are you, boy, a faggot? I tell you..."

Dimples looked at me, smiled, and covered her mouth. One thing about us, we were always laughing with each other and not *at* each other, so I knew it was her way of saying "Fuck him." It was still funny.

It hurt, and honestly, it was one of the first times he had actually been mean to me.

"No, Daddy, I'm not a faggot." I went into my room and got ready for bed.

chapter 36

The Baby

"Momma, you want me to help you with the bags?"

"Yes, please, help me, baby," Momma said.

"Momma, you want me to help with the groceries too?"

"Hell, Candy, it would take you a damn year to get down one step because of your big-ass stomach."

Candy was nine months pregnant by this time, and I'm not sure how she looked when she was pregnant with me, but this was the most noticeable thing and I wondered if they all lived full time in the world of denial.

Me and Momma were downstairs when we heard a big crash. "Momma! Help!" Candy dropped the plate of French toast she'd been munching on.

"Girl, what's wrong with you?" Momma ran back into the house with me following close behind, trying not to drop the bag of food.

"I don't know. My stomach hurts so bad, and then I peed."

"You done pissed on my couch!"

If you'll recall, Candy couldn't control when she had to go to the bathroom, but as she got older, she knew better. This wasn't pee. And Charles was the clever one who knew it.

"That girl 'bout to have her baby. Mae, call an ambulance," Charles said in the low, monotone voice he used for everything.

"Charles, can't you call? You see I got my hands full." Momma helped Candy up off the couch.

Charles dialed 911. "Hello? Can I get somebody over here at one oh nine Landon Street? I think Mae's daughter Candy is about to have a baby."

"Give me the phone." Momma snatched it from him. "What the hell kind of way is that to talk to the people?" She said into the phone, "Yes, hello, thank you, can you please send the doctor over here now?"

I sat there thinking what a fucking mess this was. And then I thought, *Wow, I am truly nothing like these people.* I started thinking that maybe, just *maybe* I was actually adopted, and Candy *did* have a tumor in her stomach, and all of it was merely a really messed-up dream.

* * *

"You can come in now," the nurse said to Momma as we sat in the waiting room at Children's Hospital.

Momma got up, a confused look on her face. "Come on, Bookie," she said. I skipped to catch up with her.

"Hi, Momma," Candy said, looking over at us with an out-of-it expression.

"You okay, baby?"

"Yeah, Momma, but it hurts down there."

Of course it hurts down there. Damn. Even to this day it still blows me away when I think about that poor thing who was only seventeen, already having had two children. I guess this was just one of the things troubling Momma. She sat there not saying much, not knowing what to say to her only daughter. But there was no time for feeling sorry for herself or anyone else. The nurse came into the room with the most beautiful little girl I had ever seen in my life. She looked just like a doll.

"Here she is," the nurse said with a smile, placing the baby in Candy's arms.

Once the nurse had gone and everyone had taken in the tiny, perfect face, Momma pulled up a chair to the side of the bed and looked straight at Candy.

"You still haven't told me whose baby this is even though I asked you time and time again."

"It's..." she hesitated. "It's John Austin's."

"Silvia's boy?"

Nadine Austin was known as the Numbers Lady on the block and ran an illegal lottery operation out of her house. Nadine was also one of the nicest people I knew, and it was me who'd run in and deliver the numbers to her. There was also a downside to her, having probably one of the nastiest houses on the block. It always looked like there was a fresh layer of dirt on everything, and her husband, who we called Poppy, looked like a silverback gorilla. The biggest, blackest man who wore nothing but thin shorts that his balls would just be hanging out of on either side. He would sit right in the middle of the couch, legs all spread, smiling a white-toothed smile. In all fairness, he was a very sweet man, as nice as Nadine, so I didn't mind running in for those twenty seconds.

"Lord," Momma said, although I think she would have said that no matter whose baby this was. "Does he know it's his, Candy?"

"No, Momma, he don't know."

"Well, good, 'cause he ain't shit, so it don't matter."

"What you gonna call her, Candy?" I asked.

"Natasha Marie," Candy said, beaming down at the face of her angel.

"Shit, don't tell John, whatever you do. I don't want his ass down at my house all the time," Momma said.

Nobody really knew this, but by that time Candy was seeing a man who always looked homeless no matter what he did. His name was

Anthony but everyone called him Tony. He was the adopted son of Reverend Jones of the Mt. Ararat Baptist Church. Tony looked like a muskrat. The boy was a mess all the time.

Momma didn't know what to think, and I could see the look on her face, even while everyone was smiling and talking about the baby. It looked like defeat, guilt, and dismay pasted all over, and I'm sure she felt like much of this was her fault. If anyone had asked me, I would have said it *was* all her fault. Her daughter, someone who couldn't fend for herself and needed her mother's protection, was ruined. Meanwhile, the things that were more important to Mae were also falling apart, but this was just the beginning.

* * *

Candy was finally home with the baby.

"Look at my little girl," Momma said, holding baby Tasha.

Candy had a puzzled look. Everyone knew Candy was slow, but she wasn't dumb, and she could feel the weird energy in the room as much as I could. It was like Momma was in a trance, holding the baby girl in her arms, walking in circles around the living room, cooing and *oohing* and *aahing*. Tasha was finally the perfect baby girl she had always wanted. She had the perfect boy in Gerry, and now there was another baby child she could spoil and raise as her own.

"That's *my* girl, Momma," Candy said feebly, knowing it was no use.

"Girl, I know this is yo baby but hell, who gonna take care of her if I don't?"

Candy just smiled the way she often did when she didn't know what to say.

"Knock, knock!" Without waiting for an answer, Willie came into the house, loud and laughing. "Where is my grandbaby?"

"I'm right here," I said.

"You sure are!" he laughed, hitting me playfully on the back of my head. "How you doing?"

Willie wasn't the smartest man, couldn't read his own name if it were written on the side of a hot air balloon, but he was pure at heart and hilarious. Willie was also pretty good-looking. Most of the men in the family were, very tall, really good-looking, but ninety percent of them were totally fucked up.

"Hey, Daddy," Candy said.

"Hey, baby, let me see this ugly little girl of yours." He laughed again, then leaned over Momma's shoulder. "Look at her! Ooh, ain't she gorgeous! Let me hold her."

"Not on your life. Your hands are dirty and I know you been drinking or something," Momma moved away from his outstretched arms.

"Give me the damn baby, Mae," he said, still smiling, but she knew not to push it with him. "All right, but be careful."

"Tasha is daddy's grand-baby," he said, looking into her beautiful face. "Where's Charles at?"

"He in his room," Momma said. "Damn, do the nigga ever come out of there?"

Everyone chuckled except for Momma. The truth hurt.

"All right, y'all, I'm heading out, I just wanted to stop by and say hello to everybody." He handed the baby back to Momma, gave everyone in the room a dollar, gave me a fiver, then left.

"I love him," I said to no one in particular as he walked out of the house. He was a simple man with good intentions.

* * *

Tony and Candy were in the living room with the baby. Tasha wasn't having a good day, irritated and crying.

"Shut that goddamn baby up! You think I wanna hear that damn fuss all night?" Charles said, coming out of the room.

I remember thinking, *It's a baby, man, what do you want them to do?*

"When Mae get back here, I'm going to let her know either y'all gonna get the hell out of here, or I am."

"I'm sorry, Daddy," Candy said, but Charles was having none of it.

"Sorry ma ass, that's all I ever hear. Sorry I'mma have another baby when I can't even wipe my own ass, sorry I can't do shit around the house, sorry I choose the shittiest fucking men to have babies with as I sit on my crippled ass like a lump on a log, sorry, sorry, sorry!" he yelled, then went back into his room.

Candy started to cry. That man was slowly turning into something terrible.

"Candy, maybe we need to go ahead and get our own place," Tony said, pulling her close to him.

"Momma ain't gon' let us take Tasha or Terrell," she said through her tears.

"*I'm* not going to let you take Terrell," I said under my breath.

"They can all come visit whenever they want," he said, trying to comfort her.

"I think it's a good idea. Let's do it." Candy smiled and looked at me as if to ask if it was okay.

How the hell do you answer something like that? I just smiled back and went into my room.

chapter 37

The Attic

"Dimples! Let's build a table over here for the experiments." I was all excited.

"Yeah, and look at this!" She showed me a couch she'd put together out of the old toy pool table and some dusty cushions. It actually looked good, and I remember thinking what a sweet girl she was. All she needed was someone to love her. Like *really* love her. Take time with her. I wondered why the women in the family never gave her that.

"Look at this, Terrell." She held up some old clothes that we were going to turn into a rug and a tablecloth.

"What y'all doing up here?" said a voice coming out of the darkness. Dimples and I jumped about a mile high.

"You scared me, man," I said, then realized it was Gerry.

Of course it was...lurking in the shadows. There we were, having some innocent fun, and this dude had to come and spoil it all.

"Y'all wanna play doctor?" Without waiting for an answer, he took out his thing and started waving it around like a windmill. We laughed uncomfortably. The laughing stopped when he grabbed Dimples and started bringing her close to him.

"Come on over here and hold it, Terrell."

"Hold it for what?" This was a genuine question, I thought he was about to take a piss. By now, I think we knew exactly what was happening, and that's crazy enough in and of itself, but when you're a kid you don't think, *Hey, I'm being abused here. This is wrong.*

Well, I did, and Dimples did as well. This fuck didn't think we knew this was wrong or weird. But we were children and those kinds of taboos like sex were still things we wondered about. What a weird mix of fear, curiosity, mistrust, and trust.

"Move it back and forth," he told me. "Don't you wanna make me feel good?"

"Don't you feel good already?"

Me and Dimples started to laugh again, thinking that was the funniest thing. In reality, we were more ashamed at having to witness this with each other than the act itself.

Then he pulled out some type of lotion from his pocket and told Dimples to turn around and started to push himself inside her like he'd tried before.

Neither of us did a thing to stop it, and while I watched him forcing himself upon her, I remember feeling like I was watching from above. There was a part of me that thought this was wrong, a part of me wanted to keep it going, and another part of me that felt like this was the love we were both so desperately searching for.

chapter 38

Another Sunday Morning

While I was getting dressed for church, the radio was playing the wonderful sounds of gospel music, as well as radio host Don Allen's boring-ass voice speaking in between, and even sometimes on top of the songs. I was always singing along with some of the songs, no matter if they were gospel or R&B.

"Hurry up, we gotta be on time," Momma said, running around the room looking for her stockings. "We getting the baby baptized today!" I handed them to her. "Thank you, Peewee."

"It's Terrell, Momma." She did that a lot, so I was actually used to it, but I always wondered why she never mixed me up with Gerry. Maybe she thought I was weak in some way like him. I realized that Gerry also represented the kind of men Momma liked.

"Okay, I got everything together. Let's go, Terrell."

We all headed to the front porch.

Granny came out and locked her door. "Here we go, I'm ready." She was wearing all white, but I guess Momma forgot it was the first Sunday.

"Hey, Granny," I said with a smile.

"How you doing, Bookie? Tit been crying this morning?"

"Who, Granny?" I said, trying to keep from laughing.

"Tit. That little baby," she said as we all loaded up into the car.

"Granny, where did you get that from?" Momma asked, also trying not to laugh. "That's what she is. A tit."

I couldn't wait until Tasha was old enough to understand the meaning of this. I couldn't wait to tease her about it.

* * *

By this time, we had gotten into a routine. Momma was a home care nurse taking care of a woman named Mrs. Gerber who she would often tell us funny stories about. Charles was home most days and out most nights since he found out that the plant was about to close, forcing him into early retirement. Candy and Tony had moved into their own place. Dimples and Tasha were sharing a room next to Momma and Daddy's, and I was in the back in what was once a closet. You had to go through my room to get to the bathroom. In our dysfunctional normalcy, birthdays, school years, and summers seemed to just fly by like a bat outta hell.

chapter 35

She's Moving In

As Dimples and I made our way back to the house around five, after swimming at the local pool, we could hear a woman's loud cackle from the corner. I recognized it immediately and when I opened the door to the house, there she was.

"Bwahahahahaha, bwahahahaha, bwahahaha! Mae, you are so crazy!"

Diane was the third daughter of Momma's sister, Aunt Louise. She lived in Chicago and Diane didn't get along with her at all. In fact, Diane didn't get along with anyone at all.

"Come over here and give your cousin a hug," Diane said to me, then looked over my shoulder before I could get a word in. "Who is this?" she asked with that megaphone of a voice she had.

"This is Dimples. She's a part of our family," Momma said. "Dimples, this is Diane, my niece."

"What, she ain't got no tongue?" Diane asked.

Dimples and I went and sat on the couch, waiting for an explanation as to why she was here with a suitcase.

"I'm going to be moving around the corner next Wednesday, so I'm going to stay with y'all until then."

I looked at Momma and she knew exactly what I was thinking. Momma could never say no to family unless it was for money.

The next morning, Momma had already left for work by the time Dimples and I got up. We decided to make breakfast.

"Let's make French toast!" Dimples said.

"Sorry y'all, I used all the eggs, bacon, and bread," Diane said, flopping down on the couch with a plate that looked like a loaf of bread, a dozen eggs, and half a pig.

"Dang, you took everything," Dimples said.

"Well there wasn't that much left," Diane said, raising her voice like Dimples had told her she was a whore. "Anyway, I can eat whatever I want, I'm family. Unlike *some* people in this room," she added harshly.

"What about me? I'm family too, but now I don't have shit to eat." Dimples and I laughed and laughed.

"Diane, you could have at least waited to see if anyone else wanted anything," Dimples said.

"I guess we'll just starve," I said.

"Bookie, who you talkin' to like that? Let that girl alone," Charles said from the bedroom door with a mean look on his face. "Sit yo mannish ass down somewhere, talkin' shit."

This was the first time I was sure his feelings for me had changed, and I don't know why this didn't really hurt me. He was the only father figure I had at the time, but for some reason I didn't let it bother me.

"Sorry, Daddy," I said.

"Sorry my ass. Sorry didn't do it," he said.

Dimples poked me and said, "Come on." She led me into the kitchen where we made a couple of bowls of cereal with what milk was left and went into my room.

* * *

"Diane is a bitch. I hated her the minute I saw her," Dimples said after she emptied her cereal bowl.

"Yeah, I know. Just think how I feel, I've had to see her my whole life," I said.

"Did you see? She took the damn food and swallowed it whole while we was trying to figure out what to do," she said. "And the worst thing about it is I'm still hungry and there ain't no more damn cereal left!"

The two of us started laughing our heads off. We couldn't hold it in any longer.

After we calmed down I said, "I don't understand how Momma can't see she's just using her."

"Yeah, and what the hell is Daddy's problem?"

"I know, right? Defending her bitch-ass like she was the Queen of Sheba. And why he just turned on me all of a sudden and started talkin' all that shit?" I slammed the empty cereal bowl down on the dresser.

"Bookie! What the hell you slammin' that damn bowl on the dresser for? If you break it you ain't got a goddamn dime to buy another!" Charles said when he passed my room on his way to the bathroom.

I looked at Dimples and our eyes got wide. We could hear him still talking shit in the bathroom.

"I really don't know what the hell his problem is," I said under my breath.

"He must be on his period," she said, and we busted out laughing again.

When we heard the toilet flush we darted out of the room towards the back door and headed straight for the attic, running up the stairs and into our makeshift apartment. We fell onto the "couch" and laughed for what seemed like an eternity.

I was so grateful for Dimples coming into my life because truly, we were all we had in that nuthouse.

chapter 40

Sweetie Pie

"Come on, children! Get all your costumes together. We gotta make it over to the nursing home before they put all of the seniors to bed!" Sweetie Pie yelled out to us kids as we were running around in our excitement.

Sweetie Pie was a sweet woman from the neighborhood who put together a group of kids to entertain some of the old folks. There would also be a few kids from the area whose grandparents were in the home. She named us Sweetie Pie's Angels, and Dimples and I had joined to get ourselves out of the house and away from Charles and Diane, who had still not moved into that infamous place around the corner.

Sweetie Pie had chosen the song "The Greatest Love of All" by Whitney Houston for me to sing and I was terrified, this being my first time singing in front of a crowd that wasn't sitting in a church. It wasn't the six old-ass members of Open Door Baptist Church, these were my peers, a lot of the young kids in the neighborhood. There was a huge threat of my ass being teased to high heaven since it wasn't popular for a boy to be singing back then. It was way before *American Idol* and *America's Got Talent*.

We started loading up the van since Sweetie Pie had us doing most of the work to learn what went into putting on a show. I think of it as my very first training as a performer.

"Stop stepping on my shoe!" one of the girls said to another.

"I can't fit in here!" one of the boys said.

"Move over! That's my seat!"

There was general chaos, just like most of these kids' home lives, ours included. Sweetie Pie knew that, so she hoped to bring a little fun and structure to some of us.

"Children, I'm going to need your cooperation," Sweetie Pie said.

Somehow, we managed to get all the props in the van and get it all together, and away we went.

* * *

When we pulled up to the nursing home. I got out of the van and looked up at the place, thinking, *Wow, you live eighty years, most of it with one trouble after the other* (if my family members were anything to go by) *and then you end up in a place like this.* It was boring, ugly on the outside, death on the inside.

Sweetie Pie must have seen the look on my face because she leaned down to me and said, "Come on, Terrell, they won't bite."

All sixteen of us filed in through back door and began preparing for the show. I could hear the crowd out there yelling and hooting and hollering, and I thought those senior citizens must be different from what I had imagined them to be when I got out of the van. The show was going great, and Sweetie Pie had decided to save me for last.

The big moment came, and Sweetie Pie said, "Terrell, are you ready?" She was already bursting with pride. Sweetie Pie saw my potential long before I even knew what the word meant.

"I'm ready," I said, then it immediately hit me. I had completely forgotten that not only a bunch of senior citizens would be out there, but a lot of my neighborhood would be there, and I almost shit myself. "Are you sure they're gonna like this?" I asked tentatively.

She looked at me reassuringly, put a hand on my shoulder, nodded, then walked me right out into the light. This was the first time I had been in front of so many people, and I was shaking, feeling like hiding behind Sweetie Pie. But there was also a part of me that was somehow ready.

"This young man is new to the angels," Sweetie Pie began. "He has a truly amazing voice, sent right from heaven, but most of all, he has such a beautiful spirit."

Some of the neighborhood boys were laughing and pointing to each other as I slowly came out from Sweetie Pie's shadow and when I saw that, God...I wanted to dart out the side door and run away. But I knew she wouldn't let that happen.

"We need to take care of our children, for they are truly the greatest love of all. Terrell! Sing!" Sweetie Pie gently nudged me forward and left the stage.

"Come on, Terrell! Sing it!" someone called from the audience.

I began to sing the opening lines of "The Greatest Love of All." The crowd cheered and fell silent.

I had sung the first few lines of what was going to take me on a remarkable journey.

* * *

After the enthusiastic crowd died down and we were all gathering behind the makeshift stage, Sweetie Pie smiled at me. "I am so proud of you, darling. You are something and someone special."

I didn't know how to react and stood there, sort of in a daze. "Thanks, Sweetie Pie," was about all I could muster.

She knelt down in front of me, took my hands, and looked directly at me. That's when I saw the tears in her eyes. "Terrell, do you hear what I'm telling you? You have a special gift, and you will bring something very important to the world." She hugged me so tight I almost couldn't breathe. "I want to thank you and God for choosing me to be the one to show this to you," Sweetie Pie said, wiping tears from her eyes.

chapter 41

Dimples's Boyfriend

After all that I was as hungry as hell, so I ran in and went straight to the kitchen.

"I guess you just nasty, walkin' right in the house and not gonna wash either hand," Charles said from the door of the bedroom. It was like he couldn't leave that place anymore, like that doorway was some kind of self-styled safety zone where he could yell all his hateful shit from. I didn't understand how he knew exactly what was going on in the kitchen at all times if he never left.

"I'm just looking, Daddy."

"Terrell, go wash your hands and change your clothes and then get something," Momma said gently, trying to make up for the venom coming out of Charles's mouth as she and Diane got ready to leave for bingo.

"Yeah, and clean 'em good," Diane added to the mix, laughing loud and hard. Diane laughed like the wicked witch of the east *and* west from the *Wizard of Oz*.

"Damn, stupid-ass boy don't know his ass from a hole in the wall," Charles said.

Here he was, coming out with another smart comment that made no sense at all, and I hadn't yet realized how it was affecting me. I've been told by friends that I have the wittiest comebacks, and with Charles and his idiocy, I got tons of practice. All of it being in my head, of course.

"Charles, can you drop us off so we won't have to find parking?" Momma asked sweetly.

"I ain't going that way. I'm going in a different direction."

"Aw, come on, Charles, if you don't take us, we gonna have to walk the whole damn way," Diane said, even sweeter.

"Oh, all right, I'll take you."

By this time, I knew exactly what the situation was and wondered how Momma didn't see it, even though that brief exchange went right over everyone else's head as well. To my mind, when your woman asks you to take her somewhere and you say no, then her loud-mouthed niece who has no job and is home with you all day long asks you and you say yes, there's got to be more to the story.

As soon as they walked out the door, Dimples came into the kitchen. "I hate her. I didn't even want to come out of my room until they left. What the hell she still doing here anyway? I thought she was moving around the corner."

"You asking me? I think it's yo daddy we need to ask." We gave each other a look. "Hell, I ain't gonna ask him. You gonna ask him?"

That's when the phone rang and startled us both. It was for Dimples.

Dimples took the phone from me and a smile came across her face. "Come on over, it's just me and Terrell here now," she said to the person on the other end.

"Who was it?"

"Sherad."

Sherad was Dimples's boyfriend. I liked the guy, and we always had a blast when he came over. She ran into the room trying to get her hair together. Dimples was such a pretty girl, but for some reason her hair never wanted to cooperate.

The doorbell rang shortly thereafter, since Sherad lived right around the corner.

"Come in, man, she's getting ready."

"What up, pretty boy?" he said. There was something about Sherad that always made me smile. He had the best energy, and I could tell he was truly interested in being cool with me. Sherad was actually the pretty boy, real good-looking with hazel eyes. Definitely a heartbreaker.

"Sherad, baby, come in here," Dimples said.

He went to her room and I went to change out of my suit, then I went back into the kitchen to cook some food. After I ate, I decided to go in and talk to Dimples and Sherad for a while, but when I got to the door, I couldn't hear them and wondered if they'd left.

I opened the door a crack and called her name, which is when I noticed they were in the process of having sex.

"Close the door, Terrell," Dimples said.

But I wanted to see this, so I stepped into the room and closed the door behind me. It wasn't like I hadn't seen Dimples have sex in front of me before, which was why it felt totally normal to me to hang out and watch the two of them get it on.

"I said get out, Terrell!" she shouted. Sherad looked back at me with a smile.

"Nope." I knew she wasn't going to stop so she could put me out, but hell if she did, then ran into the bathroom. Sherad started laughing.

"Why didn't you close the door?" Laughing, he got up, and before he went to the bathroom to check on Dimples, he took me around my neck and smiled. "You like to watch, don't you?"

Yeah, and had I been white, I would have been blushing. He didn't say anything else, and I followed him into the bathroom where he turned her around and began to have sex with her again, right in front of me.

I remember thinking this was the first time I saw any real affection from someone that made either of us feel good. The other times were forced—or in today's words "without consent"—but I could feel the love between Sherad and Dimples, and I found myself getting lost in every emotion, moan, and thought about what was going on in front of my eyes. Nothing could have broken the spell for me except when I decided to get closer so I could see better.

"Terrell, get the hell out of here!" Dimples yelled.

"Okay, playboy," Sherad said in defense of his girlfriend. He pushed me out, then slammed the door behind him.

I couldn't believe it. I couldn't stop thinking about what I was missing in that bathroom. I comforted myself with thoughts of how she must be feeling, knowing someone cared enough to make her feel the way he felt and vice versa. I wanted that feeling too, to be touched in the same way as I had seen them touch each other, to feel as if someone loved me. A thousand questions came into my head, wondering how Dimples would feel afterwards, how long they had been doing this before today, and I wanted to see more, to experience the same thing for myself. In fact, I was so lost in thought, I must not have heard the door open downstairs and the creaking of all thirteen of those old wooden stairs.

"Terrell, what the hell are you doing? Meditating?"

"Momma, when did you...how...?"

She and Diane started taking off their coats.

"I gotta pee so bad," Diane said, running to the back of the house.

"I can't believe we went all the way up there and the damn place was closed," Momma was saying when the realization hit me like a ton of bricks. Dimples was in the bathroom with Sherad!

"Mae! Get in here! You ain't gonna believe this!" Diane shouted.

Dimples and Sherad came running out of the bathroom putting on their clothes just as Momma came around the corner.

"What the fuck are y'all doing?" Momma asked, even though she knew damn well.

"I'm sorry, Momma," Dimples said.

"Get yo ass outta here," Momma said, swatting at Sherad with her bingo sticks.

He ran to the front door as fast as he could and down the stairs, leaving one of his shoes on the top ledge. Dimples went crying into her room.

"I can't wait until your father gets home," Momma said. "Just you wait."

There was no way I was coming out from under the bed.

* * *

"Is it true, Terrell? Did you see Dimples having sex with a boy in this house?" Aunty Janice asked me.

Aunty Janice was Dimples's aunt on her mother's side. She was known as a lean, mean, fighting machine kind of woman. Rumor had it she was once a Black Panther. Built like the Tasmanian Devil, buff on top, no ass, and skinny legs, she carried herself like she would spin in a minute and destroy everything in her path. I was terrified of her, based on the things that Dimples had told me, and now those fears were about to be justified.

"Y-y-yes...I did," I stuttered as Charles looked at me with the deepest of hate in his eyes.

"That's all I need to know," Aunty Janice said. She went into a whirlwind, heading in the direction of Dimples's bedroom. I feared for her and what would be left of her after this woman's wrath was unleashed.

"What—the—hell—were—you—doing—with—a—boy—in—this—damn—room?!" she yelled, swatting Dimples with a belt, a stick, and a shoe with each word.

"I'm sorry, Aunty, I won't do it again!" Dimples sobbed.

"Damn right you won't, 'cause yo ass gonna be so red ain't no one gonna wanna get near it!"

I felt so bad for her, but there was nothing I could do to help.

The beating went on for a least another half hour until she finally decided to let Dimples rest.

"Next time you'll think twice before doing stupid-ass shit like that."

All nonchalant, everyone pretended to watch TV as Aunty Janice gathered her things. "Mae, I'm sorry for disrupting your household like that, but this is my sister's child, and someone needs to whip her ass for that since her own momma ain't gonna do it."

"I know, that's right, Janice," Momma said.

I sat there wondering, *Why, all of a sudden, are we being punished for underage sex? Damn.*

"I know you had something to do with it," Daddy said to me, giving me the evil eye as he retreated back into the bedroom.

I look back now and see that we weren't loved even by the standards of the worst parents, which was where my warped sense of love and affection was born. Even though Charles hated me, and it was now very apparent, I didn't care. I couldn't stop thinking about the look on Dimples and Sherad's faces in that bathroom and the feelings I was experiencing, knowing she was being touched like that, with all the love flowing. All the love...in spite of all the hate.

chapter 42

Ujima Theater Company

After a while, I started singing at places around the city. The other advantage to getting out of the house and away from all the toxicity was that I began to learn more about my voice. Someone invited me to see a show at an urban theater called the Ujima Theater Company, which was well known in the Upstate New York area for its edgy, entertaining musicals.

The show at the small theater, *In the Beginning*, written by the late, great, Oscar Brown Jr. was an adaptation of the Adam and Eve story, with a slight urban twist. The opening music started to play, and the singers came out with a powerful number called "One Life." The voices were amazing. I was so excited I could hardly keep myself in my seat. It was at that moment that I knew this was something I wanted to do. They were good, but I knew even then that I could do this just as well, if not better.

When the show was over, I waited around to meet the director and the owner of the theater company, Lorna Hill.

"Hi! My name is Terrell and I want to be a singer," I said. "I loved the show and was wondering if there was a way I could come and volunteer here?"

"Actually, yes, we always have room for young people who want to be in the arts. Can you start tomorrow?"

"I can! I'll come up right after school." I left the theater and shouted out loud as I walked home, "I'm going to be a star! *I'm going to be a star!*" I didn't even want to catch the bus, I decided I would walk... or fly home.

* * *

I flew into the house, singing a song from the show at what I thought was a whisper, when I heard that familiar voice coming from the bathroom.

"Shut yo ignorant ass up. I can't even take a shit in this house without you whoopin' and hollerin'."

"Sorry, Daddy I was just singing one of the songs I heard at—"

"If you call that shit singin' you must be crazy."

I started walking into my room slowly, thinking the best thing to do was just ignore him, but my mouth opened before I could stop myself and I said, "Shut up, bitch."

"I *know* you didn't just call me a bitch, boy," Charles said.

"No, I did not." I started to close the door to my room when Charles stuck his foot out so I couldn't.

"You need somebody to bust them big lips for you."

Momma came out of the bedroom and for once defended me from Charles, simply by putting her hands on her hips and giving him a look.

I went into my room and thought about how I didn't know if I had more fear of him or of what was happening. I always felt like my life wasn't right and knew deep down that the rest of the world couldn't possibly be dealing with the unbearable life I had. With shows like *The Cosby Show, The Jeffersons,* and *Good Times* giving us mixed signals on how life was, and, if you worked hard, could be, I always had it in my mind that there was something else, some other place that was better than where I was. Another life that was better than the life I sure as shit didn't ask for. Holding onto the hope that there was a better tomorrow, feeling like an alien that had landed on another planet with no instruction book, I pushed on and through it all, feeling I was so much greater than this. Which was exactly what pissed Charles off, I think. A life greater than what his was, living where he didn't want to be, with no hope of getting out.

I had hope. And it would be with music and performing. The next days at school were unbearable for my homeroom teacher Mr. Tritto, seeing me sitting at my desk, staring out the window.

"Terrell! What planet are you on? Terrell?"

In those last few weeks, I couldn't think of anything else but theater, music, and singing. I was lost in a world of harmonies and make-believe, and somehow, I knew this would be the world I would live in for the rest of my life. In fact, my world was about to change even more, and I although I loved volunteering at the Ujima Theater Company, soon I wouldn't have time to do it.

chapter 43

Lighthouse

I was starting to sing at churches more and more around the city, always with my friend Tony Robinson on piano. There were so many other singers who could really sing, but I knew I had something different. Finished with imitating singers like Stevie Wonder and Aretha Franklin, I started cultivating my own sound. However, I knew I had a long way to go and realized I needed to be singing as much as possible.

One day after singing at Mt. Ararat Baptist Church for a Sunday night concert, Marsha Davidson, another singer who had performed that evening, told me about a group she'd heard of. Marsha, known as one of the city's dope sopranos, had a high range and didn't mind using it.

"Did you hear that group tonight? The Lighthouse Interdenominational Choir?" she asked me.

"Oh, Lord, did I," I answered.

They were a group of people around the music scene I'd never seen in Buffalo before, and there were a lot of young people in it. Marsha thought it would be a good idea if we talked to the leader of the group to see if they were letting people join.

We approached the director of the group, Minister Jerome L. Ferrell, a heavy-set, animated character who was hilarious. In fact, you wanted to laugh just looking at him.

"Hello, Minister Ferrell, my name is Marsha Davidson, and this is my friend Terrell Carter. We were wondering if you were holding auditions for Lighthouse anytime soon?"

Jerome looked up with a face of importance and said, "Well, can you sing?"

We both nodded enthusiastically. "Yes!"

"We both sang solos today," Marsha told him.

Jerome was a star around Buffalo and all the surrounding areas, and was the only person actively recording and making moves in the gospel world...and he didn't let you forget it. "We're having auditions this Thursday at our rehearsal if you want to stop by. How old are you, young man?" he asked, looking me up and down. "Our minimum age is sixteen."

I wouldn't be sixteen until the next year, but I wasn't about to pass up this opportunity. "I'm sixteen, sir." Yes, I know, lying right there in the church in front of God and everybody.

"Come by around four o'clock."

"We'll see you there," Marsha said, and before we could even shake his hand, he was off to the next person praising him for that night's fabulous performance.

* * *

That evening as I lay in bed, I couldn't help but wonder why I felt so lonely. I had the most amazing opportunities coming my way, and I was going for them on my own without help from anyone, but for some reason I kept thinking about all the things that *weren't* right in my life. It was a feeling of dread that would haunt me for years to come, wondering if anyone really cared if I lived or died. After all, I was a *mistake*. I would ask God for an answer, praying to him to give me the reason for my existence. As I closed my eyes and drifted off to sleep, I thought, *I suppose I will understand it better "In the by-and-by" as Granny used to say.*

* * *

Tuesday rolled around and I showed up right on time at the Lighthouse Choir rehearsal.

"Okay, folks, we have two new people who would like to join us," Jerome said, flopping down in the raggedy chair that was placed at the front of the church. You could tell it was his favorite because it had wheels on it, and he would zip all over the front of the church with it. Jerome was a heavy-set man, as animated as a cartoon character. Everyone clapped and applauded for me and Marsha. "I'm going to ask them to sing, so ladies first."

Marsha came to the front of the church and started her song. *"If the lord…"*

I don't know what went wrong, but there was a crack, followed by a complete train wreck. The keyboard player looked at the drummer and they both laughed, without Marsha noticing, thankfully. I was more sure than ever about my gift at this time, but even still, I got *so* nervous.

"Thank you, honey, that's enough," Jerome said. "We appreciate you taking the time but it's less than what we are looking for. Don't give up! Practice some more and come back next year." As kind as his delivery was, there is no way to not feel a bit weird in front of twenty or thirty of the best singers in Buffalo. I felt so sorry for Marsha, especially since it was because of her that I was even standing there. In a flash, she grabbed the mic and started an a cappella song in a key that was high enough for dogs to hear. Her voice soared all over the church and everybody clapped when the musicians started playing towards the end.

When she was finished, Jerome said, "Why didn't you do that from the start? Go ahead and take a seat in the soprano section."

Marsha made it! Now it was my turn.

Jerome handed me the mic. "Terrell, what are you going to sing for us?"

Without waiting for the musicians to begin, I started singing, "His Eye Is on The Sparrow."

The entire place was silent after I was finished. I stood there feeling a bit awkward until Jerome stood up and, putting his hands together in prayer, said, "Oh my heavens, what a voice, and what range!" He glanced briefly at the other members of the choir, then back to me. "I want to welcome you to the Lighthouse Interdenominational Choir, Terrell Carter."

The house erupted and everyone cheered, then came down to greet me and introduce themselves to me and Marsha. This couldn't have come at a better time. The theater company wasn't doing any shows and I was one more step closer to my dream.

* * *

I ran into the house singing at the top of my lungs. "Yes! I'm a believer!"

"Shut yo damn mouth, you stupid-ass boy," Charles said to me when I almost ran into him coming out of the bathroom where I swear to God he spent most of his time. "Damn, when you in the house can't nobody get no damn rest," he mumbled. "I hate yo ass, y'all get on my damn nerves."

I went into my room and closed the door. It was amazing how that man could destroy my mood with merely a few words. I pulled out the tape I had hidden behind the television. Over the past few months I had grown increasingly dependent on the porn tapes I had stolen from Peewee. You see, the love I had witnessed between Dimples and Sherad was a love I wanted for myself, and I wanted it *so* badly, I would take it any way I could get it. I started stealing porn tapes then bringing them back, putting them in his collection and hoping he wouldn't notice. I'd sit there watching until I fell asleep.

This was around the time I began to develop dependencies on various items and feelings. Not only porn, I found myself leaning on anything that made me feel good: sugar, people, music—and all forms of love—or what felt and looked like love. Fortunately, it wasn't drug or alcohol abuse, but it was when my trust issues began. I always thought, if the people who were supposed to love me unconditionally could treat me this way, how could someone that I meet be trusted? Having nothing to base normal behaviors on, I just did whatever felt good to me. There were times when I found myself in situations with people where it was sexual for them, but for me it was the truth of just wanting to feel loved. There were older women and men who would see me at church, sometimes even those people pretending to mentor, and would try to maneuver me into some sexual situations, but being as cognizant and aware of my surroundings as I was, most of the time I'd see it coming. I always thought how funny it was that Candy was special needs, but I was especially sharp. These feelings and dependencies were some that I would be fighting off for the rest of my life. Having had virtually no guidance or discipline, I was left to figure things out on my own. Not easy when you are surrounded by total dysfunction.

Charles was becoming more and more hateful, driving a wedge between everyone. We were all afraid of him and tried to make him happy, or at least keep him from going off. I hated seeing Momma live in such torment. I could tell she was simply existing and not enjoying the prime of her life. In fact, we all were.

chapter 44

Kmart

I hadn't seen much of Candy for a while, but she always wanted to give me fifteen or twenty dollars when she got her check on the third of the month, and she would make sure to call me to meet with her and Tony.

Candy cashed her check at the check-cashing place, and we started walking back outside to Momma's car. It was always like Christmas when Candy got paid, and people would come out of the woodwork. If you'll remember, Jabo's lawyer had found a way for Momma to get Jabo's pension checks transferred to Candy after he died, so Momma felt she had a right to that money.

"Listen, Candy, I gotta make my car payment and I wanna put some of it away for you, so you need to give me half of it."

I knew if Momma got her hands on any of that money it would never be seen again.

"Okay, Momma," Candy said, still sounding like a seven-year-old, and handed her half the cash.

Candy didn't have much in the way of responsibilities because her bills were taken care of and her kids were with Momma, so everybody knew that the money was for her to burn. Which was what always happened. By the fourth, sometimes even on the evening of the third, that money was gone.

"Let's go to Kmart!" Momma said and we all piled into the car. This was the closest thing to a family outing we had, mainly because Charles hated Kmart and Diane was definitely not invited.

* * *

For me, Momma, and Candy, shopping at Kmart was always fun. I would be able to pick out a few things and Candy would buy them for me, in addition to the cash she slipped into my hand. I always tried to find things that didn't look like they were from Kmart because the bullying would be incessant. They had to be things I could wear all the time that no one would notice.

"Terrell, what you getting?" Candy asked, walking on her wooden leg from side to side. I remember looking at her and smiling, thinking this was the weirdest situation. Here was my mother, who seems like my sister, but buying me things like my mother, communicating with me like a sister, and my *little* sister at that.

"I wanna get these pants and these two shirts. Is that okay?" I asked.

"You can get whatever you want, just don't tell Momma." Candy gave me fifty more dollars. "You ma boy and you can have whatever you want."

"Look, Momma, that lady has a leg like a pirate," a little boy said as he and his mother approached from the other end of the aisle.

Candy looked over at the boy and giggled. "I sure do."

"Yeah, and I'll make your ass walk the plank if you don't get outta here," I said in my mother's defense.

The boy's mother shoved him along down the aisle. "Come on, Tommy, your dad is over here," she said with a nervous expression.

Even though we weren't on the East Side, there was still a notice-able difference between black folks and white folks, and this kind of thing didn't help.

We met up with everyone at the register so Candy could pay for their things, and while we waited, I couldn't help thinking of how it must be for her. Everywhere she went, someone was staring at her or making fun of her. Most of the time she didn't know, or it went right over her head. I guess now, looking back, her mental state was more a protection than it was a problem.

chapter 45

Oh, Shit!

Time went by and Diane was *still* living with us, devouring loaves of bread and dozens of eggs in one sitting. We never understood why she never got fat, or why she never seemed to move into that "apartment around the corner." If that wasn't crazy enough, something else weird happened. Like that would be a surprise in this family? Betty and Peewee started a relationship and decided to move in together. I'd always looked at them as cousins, but they were merely two more people from these same two families who decided to get together. I'm sure you're saying to yourself right now, "Damn, was there no one else in Buffalo they could have dated?" Trust me, I've asked myself the same thing many times.

I liked to go over there and spend weekends with them. Betty and I had such an amazing relationship, even though she could be a bit unpredictable, or in modern terms, bipolar. I'm not even sure that was a term in the eighties, back then you were just known as being crazy as hell. Now that I think about it, this was when she was just getting started with mind sickness. I was over there one particular weekend and Betty happened to be at work, so me and Peewee were hanging out.

Peewee had this habit of watching large amounts of porn, and one morning when I was showering for the day, I walked into the sitting room to get myself dressed while he was rewinding some VHS tape. I looked closer and saw a naked-ass woman and some dude.

He settled into his seat and pressed play. My eyes were glued to the television.

"So I couldn't believe it," the lady on the TV said. *"I walked into the room looking for my friend and there she was, on the pool table, and he was fucking her...in the ass!"*

Peewee and I burst out laughing. I don't know why we thought that was so hilarious. Maybe because she said it in such a proper white-lady way.

"Fawn, my man, this is crazy, ain't it?" Peewee said.

Okay, here we go again. I don't know when Peewee gave me this nickname or why, I never questioned it. I just thought this was cool, watching porn with my uncle, not realizing that this was actually an issue, and something I was too young to process. After all, it was nothing I hadn't already seen live a bunch of times before.

"What in the hell is this shit?" The door slammed and we both looked guilty, as if we had been caught stealing. Betty was pissed, standing in the room like a bull in front of the only exit.

"Oh, I—I was just rewinding this for my friend to come and pick up," Peewee lied.

"What the hell are you doing? Jerking off on my couch?" She slammed her jacket down.

I wasn't going to say one word, and although I was enjoying the video like an adult, here is where I played the role of the poor, victimized child. I looked up at her all innocent-eyed, as if I were finally glad someone with authority had come and made an adult decision in the house.

"Peewee, what in the hell you thinking, having that boy watching that?"

"Betty, I told you I wasn't watching it. Anyway, he a man, he gonna see this sooner or later. Damn, woman."

That was right about the time a flowerpot flew across the room and hit the wall. I ran for cover, and so did Peewee.

"Get yo shit and get the hell out of here," Betty said.

I sat down, refusing to even look in his direction. I had chosen sides, and it wasn't Peewee's. Poor Peewee. He'd only moved in two weeks before.

chapter 46

The French Toast Incident

The "French Toast Incident" happened a few months after Diane began her eating spree through our home. I was at the point where I just couldn't take it anymore, and when it happened, I finally realized just whose home it actually was. (Hint: not mine.)

I came out of my bedroom to get me and Dimples some breakfast and there she was, sitting in front of the TV watching Good Morning America, a plate full of food on her lap, so full the plate was bent.

"Not sure there's any bread left," she said with triumph, being the bitch she was used to being.

"I'm surprised you're not fat, the way you eat all that food of ours. But then again, you've been working off this food somehow, and no one else here seems to notice but me," I said as I slapped the plate out of her hands.

"Charles! Terrell slapped my food out of my hand!" And then she started picking up that shit off the dirty-ass carpet and putting it all back on her plate.

"What in the hell!" he yelled as he came into the living room.

Now, to him, it really didn't matter what I did. Even if she had done something really wrong and had decapitated me in the process, he would have found a way to make it my fault. This man hated my black ass with a passion.

"You need somebody to bust them big lips for you, that's what you need. And I'm right here, ready to serve," he went on as he walked slowly back to the door of the bedroom, leaning against the door frame while still looking at me. Charles had a way of saying things that would hurt, but in all actuality were funny as hell when you thought about them. Who tells a kid, hell, or an adult for that matter, "You need somebody to bust them big lips for you"?

"Hahahahahaha...." I said internally, but what I did was look at him and walk out of the house. Dimples had the sense to leave, too, otherwise she was gonna be late for school. Better being hungry for school rather than late.

"Don't be cutting yo damn eyes at me, I'll knock 'em out yo goddam head," and spit came flying out of his mouth as he said it. I told you he hated my ass, no one talks so hard that spit comes out of their mouth unless they mean it!

"I am so sorry," I said, knowing full well that saying sorry to Charles was the same as calling him an asshole.

"Sorry my ass," He spewed *and* I saw the fire in his eyes. I could hear Dimples in the other room, getting her school stuff together while trying to keep her giggles under her breath. "This ain't funny, Moselle [which is, of course, Charles's nickname for her] When Mae get here, I'm gonna tell her she gotta get yo faggot ass outta here. Today."

Now listen, even though his words were harsh, this shit was funny to us. Or maybe it was the only way we could get through it. But truth be told, at the time, I never knew how much all of it affected me. How many walls and mazes I would have to tear down and go through later in life just to be able to survive.

* * *

The shit hit the fan right after school as soon as I opened the door.

"Terrell, what the hell did you do to Charles?" Momma asked.

"I didn't do anything to Charles, Momma. I was fighting with Diane because she ate all the bread again, and you know how she is with her freeloading self," I said with an attitude, even though I was caught off guard.

"Look, I can't stand all this tension, so you just gonna have to go and live with Betty or Oda-Lee until Charles finds another place."

This hurt me more than anything thus far in my life. Here I was just turning fifteen years old and my own grandmother, who for all intents and purposes was a mother to me, was telling me to leave until this grown-ass man found himself a place to live. Y'all know how long it took him last time when he was living with Mae and Jabo, and everyone knew this would never happen, so it was just her way of letting me know that if she was gonna have to choose between the two of us, it was gonna be Charles. This was the beginning of our end and the start of me growing to hate Momma.

I went into my room and sat on the bed. There was nothing I could say. There was nothing anyone could say. Even Dimples couldn't make me feel better when she came in and sat down next to me. I remember feeling so bad, a lump of shit in the middle of the floor would have looked like a prize. I got up and packed my clothes, stuffing everything I could carry into a bag, then left and caught the bus to Anie's. When she answered the door, I dropped everything and broke into tears.

chapter 47

Tables Turned

I had been living at Anie's house for a little over three months, and as much as I loved her, it wasn't easy to live in a small two-bedroom apartment with a senior citizen who was set in her ways and filled her entire place with knick-knacks. For one thing, she had these ceramic dolls, dogs, and cats placed at the center of a glass table in the living room, and when you just walked by them, they all shook and moved around like they would fall any second. Another problem was the phone situation. There was only one, with a very short cord, and it was next her to her bed. She said it was in case something happened to her and she wouldn't be able to get up to call the doctor. Never mind if she tripped and fell in the shower....

Any time I wanted to talk to my friends on the phone, I had to sit at the side of her bed. One day I came home from school, and there was a new phone in the living room with the long-ass cord that could reach all over the house.

"This is so you won't bother me when I'm trying to watch *Wheel of Fortune*," Anie said with a sly grin. She was always so sweet to me.

Even when I made her mad, I was still her baby. Except now that was getting ready to be tested.

Back then, we had discovered three-way calling, and so I was on the phone having a lively conversation with two of my friends, laughing and talking about church and who was and wasn't a good singer. I decided to get some water out of the refrigerator and was about to tell them to hold on when I remembered the long cord on the phone. I stood up, and all of a sudden I heard a loud crash. When I turned back, I saw that the cord had grabbed ahold of one of the ceramic dogs and slammed it down onto the glass coffee table so hard that the whole entire table shattered into a million pieces and everything came crashing to the floor—dogs, cats, dolls, and all.

"Holy shit. I gotta go, y'all." I slammed the phone down, not a minute too soon.

Anie came running out of her bedroom. "What in the devil's name was that?"

I knew she was going to be upset, but the wrath of Zeus came over her, and she used words I had never heard her use.

"What in the fuck are you in here doing?" she screamed at the top of her lungs. "Oh, my poor babies! Terrell, damn you, you just fuckin' up my whole goddamned house. I should have never put that damn phone in here. Why don't you go back over to Mae's and fuck *her* shit up!"

I didn't know how to respond, and I couldn't get around her to hide, so I just stood there staring at the mess until she went back in her room. It was more the shock that she had spoken to me that way than anything else. I guess the saying is true, if you want to make someone your enemy, move in with them.

* * *

After cleaning up the mess as best I could, I sat in my room for about an hour, still in a state, when I heard her slippers scooting towards my door. Anie peeked her head around the door.

"I'm sorry, Terrell, I didn't mean to go off on you, you just don't know how much that table meant to me." She sat down next to me on the bed and put her hand on my leg. "That was Jabo's table, one of the last items I got from the house before Bonnie came and took everything else."

"Oh, Anie, I'm so sorry. I didn't mean to break it."

"I know you didn't, son. It was an unhappy accident. So don't you worry about it, I'll get another." She slowly got up and went back into her room, where she started looking at pictures of Jabo and getting all melancholy.

What Anie didn't know was that I clearly remember Gerry brought that table with him from New York to give to Momma. Only Momma didn't want to keep it at the house because there were too many kids running around there, so she asked Anie to hold onto it for her. Anie was a few things, but mainly she was sweet, feisty, and a complete drama queen. I shook my head and let her sift through the pictures and make her old lady comments like, "Lord, have mercy," and "My, my, my," and "Bless us all, Jesus."

chapter 48

Lunch Time

"Bookie!" I heard loud and clear from behind me as the lunch lady handed me my tray. The lunch lady was a friend of Granny's, which was why she called me Bookie. No one else but Granny called me that.

I was in a great mood today and it was made even better because they had fried chicken and biscuits for lunch. If this wasn't a setup for eating terribly as an adult, I don't know what was. Dimples went whizzing by, laughing loudly, and I immediately started laughing too. If there was one person who could make me laugh, it was Dimples. Everyone used to say all the time that we were so much alike, and we were.

"How you doing, boo?" she asked.

"I'm all right. Just trying to survive mothballs and guilt-trips over at Anie's."

"You so damn stupid, Terrell," she laughed. "I sure miss yo ass. But hell, that shit that happened between you and Daddy that day...he just say anything, the fool, don't he?"

"Dimples, you know what it was, that damn Diane. I'm surprised Momma hasn't figured the shit out by now."

"It is truly the most dysfunctional shit ever." Dimples clicked open the top on her soda.

"Daddy just can't stand me at all and it's yo damn fault."

"*My* fault? Well!" Dimples said, clutching her fake pearls like she was some appalled white lady.

"Yes, it's yo fault since you was always in trouble and everybody talked so much shit about you, he just got tired of my sangin' ass."

She screamed with laughter. "Oh my god, Terrell, I love you so damn much. You so damn stupid."

When we got together it was like we were all alone in the world, a world that was against us, and although I had created a monster, she had taken it to another level. We could say some of the meanest shit to people and each other, and everything was funny. I realize now that it was our way of coping with it all.

"Okay look, I'm on my period and I don't want y'all to say shit to make me laugh," Charmaine Cooke said, coming up to the table.

"Well sit yo ass down and shut up then," I said even before her seat got warm. We all laughed, and laughed loudly.

"The least they could have done was make some mac and cheese," Tameka Green said, flopping down in a seat across from me.

Tameka and I had known each other since kindergarten, but for some reason I was closer to Charmaine. Probably because she got me and laughed at everything I said.

"Did y'all hear what happened to Tara?" Tameka asked.

"No, bitch, and we could care less," Charmaine answered, and we roared with laughter yet again.

"I can't stand her ass. She talk too damn much. Oh, all right, what happened?" I said right after, hoping it was something we all could get a good laugh out of.

"They caught her and Robert on the fourth floor, blowin' her back out," Tameka said.

"Shut. Up. Tameka, you lyin'." Charmaine leaned in for more information.

"I am not. They said Mister Pico caught them."

"Lord no," Charmaine said.

Mr. Pico was a heavy white teacher who was militant but funny to us all at the same time. "Yes, look around and you'll notice they ain't nowhere to be seen," Tameka said with authority.

"Hell, I haven't been looking for them," I said.

Dimples was always a bit quiet when they came around, seeing that she was a year behind us and they loved me so much. I like to think she enjoyed the banter. The bell rang and the rush out of the cafeteria began.

"Don't push me, dammit," Tameka said to me jokingly as we all left. Lunch was always the highlight of the day.

* * *

After school I went by Granny's house to get some clothes because I had Lighthouse rehearsal that night, and I needed one of my shirts, hoping Charles wouldn't be there when I got there. But of course he was, walking around with his pajamas on at four in the afternoon, back and forth to the kitchen and bathroom looking like a zombie, chewing on some of his favorite burnt-on-the-outside, raw-on-the-inside chicken.

"What the hell you doin' in that kitchen, boy? Wash the damn dishes this time if you cook something."

I hadn't been there in awhile, but it didn't matter, he just had to say something besides, *"Hey, Terrell, how are you? How you doin'?"*

I collected the things I needed and left as quickly as I could.

* * *

Jerome opened the rehearsal with a prayer and then made an announcement to everyone with a big grin.

"I've got some news for all y'all. We've just been asked to perform in Los Angeles at one of the biggest gospel conventions in the country next spring."

He paused to let that sink in and when it did, we were all blown away. In that moment it felt like we'd made it. Not only would we be performing for the people outside Buffalo, we would be singing for folks on the other side of the country! As far as me and my world was concerned, it might as well have been on the other side of the universe.

"In addition, Jester Hairston will be taking us on a tour of the NASA Space Center," he added.

Jester Hairston! He played Rolly on the show *Amen* and was regarded as a legend and leading expert on Negro spirituals and choral music. For me, this whole trip was a dream come true, and little did I know, it was the start of me outgrowing Buffalo.

Amen was the hit television show that Sherman Hemsley (George Jefferson) went to after *The Jeffersons*. The theme song was sung by none other than the sultry voice of Vanessa Bell Armstrong, a gospel legend who could do pretty much anything with her voice.

"The cost of the trip will be five hundred dollars per person, and for all of you new members, you will have to buy a robe as well as all of the necessary outfits before then." Jerome rambled off all of the details of the trip.

My heart sunk as I realized there would be no way in hell I was going to be able to get that money. I had no job, and I certainly couldn't ask anyone from home for money. There was one thing I knew for sure, though. I would definitely figure out a way to make it work.

chapter 49

Horror Night

I decided to go over to Betty's for the weekend to give Anie a break, relax, watch horror movies, and eat pizza and wings from La Nova pizza. They had the best damn wings and pizza in the city, and later as I traveled around the world, I realized there was nothing like this place.

Betty was getting all the movie choices together for us. She had over six hundred VHS tapes with horror movies on all of them. This was where my horror movie fetish came from.

"Terrell, I got three good movies I know you haven't seen," Betty said as she opened the door for the pizza man. This was during one of her and Peewee's on-again, off-again dysfunctional relationship quirks. They were off, so he had moved out and it was just her. I liked it that way because then there was less chance of them arguing or some weird shit happening. "So Momma told me you were going to be going out to California to sing for the show *Amen*."

I thought about correcting her, but it didn't matter because once things were funneled through Anie, there would definitely be some miscommunication.

"Yes, I'm excited about it." I settled down on the couch with my blanket.

"You know you are going to be a star, right?"

This was something they would say to me all the time, so I laughed.

"Yup, I sure am."

"You know I used to live out in California with my husband Willie Griffin," she said.

"Yes, I remember the time when you weren't around for a while."

A cloud came over her head as she thought about the time she had there with him. Betty never told us much about what happened with her and Willie, but I heard Anie talking one day about it to somebody on the phone. I think he abused her in every way possible. There was something that was different about Betty when she came back. She was okay but not always there, or like something was about to click at any time. These days we call it "bipolar." Back then, black people didn't know anything about that shit. We just said you were crazy and left it at that.

"Yeah, California is a beautiful place. Palm trees and sunshine all the time. It's nothing like this hellhole, with snow and shit. Buffalo doesn't even compare," Betty said.

"Wow, I can imagine that. It looks nice on the movies," I said.

"Movies don't even do it justice. I don't think you have any idea about where you're going, Terrell. I see it as plain as day. You're going to lead a life way more exciting than this dead-end shit we're all doomed for."

What do you say after someone describes their life like that? Exactly. Nothing. And that's what I said.

"Anyway, this movie is called *Something Wicked This Way Comes*, and it's going to scare the shit outta you."

I took a wing out of the box and sat back on the couch. Even though the rest of the night was filled with scary movies and those BBQ wings until we both passed out, I couldn't help thinking about what she had said to me. I could feel it inside that there was something else out there for me. I was bigger than Buffalo, and every day I would see it more and more.

chapter 50

She's Gone

I was sitting in Mrs. Cercone's boring-ass science class about to fall asleep, until a hall monitor stuck his head inside the classroom and whispered something to Mrs. Cercone.

"Damon, please go to the office," Mrs. Cercone said in the same boring tone she taught us science.

I didn't even bother to ask why, I just happily jumped up, gathered all my things, and ran off to the office.

"Hey," I said to one of the office ladies who were always so pleasant. "I was told to come down."

She looked at me sympathetically. "Yes, Damon. I'm sorry, but you need to go down to Buffalo General. Apparently, your grandmother is quite ill."

If you haven't noticed by now, one of the problems in my family is that none of them are actually called by who they really are, so it could be anyone in the hospital.

"Okay, thank you." I walked down to my locker, wondering who it was and what was really wrong. I also thought that since Betty worked at Buffalo General, if she was there today, she'd let me know what was happening.

I made the short three-block walk to the hospital, surprisingly not even thinking about how serious it could be. All I could think about were the songs I needed to learn for Lighthouse and the trip to California. That's all I could ever think about, really. I still didn't have the money, but I hadn't lost hope.

When I arrived at the door of the hospital, I saw a sweet, familiar face coming out of the front door. It was Sweetie Pie. I couldn't believe it! I hadn't seen her in years. I was so happy to see her, and she looked exactly the same as she had ten years before.

"Sweetie Pie! How are you?"

"Darling, oh my goodness, I've missed you so much. Look at my boy, all grown up now!"

"I'm gonna be sixteen soon."

"Please tell me you're still using that beautiful voice of yours," she said excitedly.

"I sure am. In fact, I'm singing in the Lighthouse Choir and we're about to go to California. If I can raise the five hundred dollars I need to go, that is."

"You mean Jerome Ferrell's choir? I *love* them. Mind you, I haven't seen them perform in a while. My husband's been ill, and I spend a lot of time here at the hospital, but..."

Suddenly I remembered why I was there. "Oh, Sweetie Pie, I'm sorry, I need to get into the hospital, my grandmother is sick."

"Oh, Terrell, I'm so sorry. I won't keep you, but please keep in touch with me. I would love to hear you sing again."

I promised her I would and ran into the hospital.

"Boy, get yo ass in this damn hospital," a voice complained. "Out here talkin' and y'all grandmother sick."

It was Aunt-Sister. Yes, her name was Aunt-Sister. She was Momma's older sister who looked just like Granny, which was why Momma called her that, and no matter how old she got, she never changed.

"Oh, so it *is* Granny," I said, somewhat confused.

"Of course it's Granny. How many grandmothers do you got?"

I decided not to get into a debate and instead walked with her to the elevator.

"What's going on with Granny, Aunt-Sister?"

"She was laying in bed over at yo Aunt Ruby's house for two days, not telling anyone she was in pain or something was wrong."

"How is she now?"

"She ain't really with it right now from what they told me."

When we got off the elevator and went into the waiting room, it was like a family reunion. Gerry, Peewee, Momma, Candy, Uncle Neil, and so on, and so on. I walked right up to Momma and didn't even acknowledge Charles.

"Momma, how is she?"

"Right now they are trying to figure it all out, but you need to go in and see her because you may not have a chance after today."

"Okay, Momma."

"Me and Peewee are going in with you," Gerry said. I didn't like it, but I didn't have a choice. We walked up the short hallway into the room where Granny was. I at least wanted to walk in first, so I squeezed ahead of Gerry. The three of us just looked down at her lying there unresponsive, with all the tubes hooked up to her mouth.

"Look like it's only a matter of time now, huh?" Gerry said.

I glared at him and my mouth almost dropped to the floor. I then said in the lowest voice I could, "What the hell is your problem?"

"What?"

"How do you know she can't hear you?"

"Well how the hell you know she can?"

I didn't. But when I looked back down at her, something told me she could. She also knew as well as I did that Gerry was one of dumbest people on the face of this Earth, so it might not have surprised her to hear him say that about someone who was clearly dying. He and Peewee walked out of the room after that and left me alone with her.

I walked over to the bed and took her hand. "Granny, who knows if you can hear me, but if you can, I wanted to say..." She pinched my finger. It shocked me a bit, because they had said she was almost gone. "You can hear me?" I said, and she pinched my finger again. It was all I could do to hold back my tears. I didn't expect to be able to talk to her again or tell her anything, and I didn't know how much time I had. "Granny, I love you and I'm here with you, now and always. You need to know how much you've meant to me over the years, how much you taught me. I'll never forget painting the house with you and laughing at all the funny things you would say. I never had to wonder how you felt about me, you always had a way of just making things right, looking on the bright side of everything and everyone. It means the world to me that I was chosen to be a part of your life." She pinched my finger again.

By now the tears were flowing, and through my own, I could see one of hers coming out of those peacefully closed eyelids. "Granny, I'm gonna miss you more than you will ever know. No matter where I go or who I'm with, I will always remember the beautiful lady who reminded me time and time again that God doesn't make mistakes." I kissed her on the cheek, and when she pinched my finger again, the light on the machine did something different and made some beeping noises.

The nurses came in and pulled me away from her, then drew the curtain around her. I could tell she was gone, and they knew it as well, which was why they didn't try and revive her like you see in the movies. One of them escorted me out of the room and back into the waiting area.

Then it hit me. I lost Granny. I sunk to the floor in the hallway and cried my eyes out. "I'll be okay," I told the nurse. "Go ahead and tell the others."

"Okay, honey." The nurse went into the waiting room and broke the news to the family.

For them to be ones that never said "I love you" and rarely showed emotion, I knew the exact moment she told them that Granny was gone because it sounded like someone threw a hand grenade into the room. Wailing and crying came in like thunder.

"Oh, lord, not my momma!"

That was all I could make out because the rest was screams and cries of pain and discomfort. They all started coming out into the halls, crying and wailing, and it was the first time I had even seen some of these ugly-ass people. Remember, Granny had seventeen children, one hundred and twenty grandchildren, and three hundred great-grandchildren. They weren't all there, but there were people I had no idea who the hell they were. One thing I do remember was that it really hurt to see so many people hurting and crying and how sad it was that it took something like this to finally bring us all together.

chapter 51

The Funeral

I hate funerals. I mean, honestly, who doesn't? But this particular one I was sure to hate more than most. Usually they are filled with people who weren't even close to the person who died or are just there to spectate. A lot of the time, the loudest person is the one who hadn't talked to the deceased person in years. Knowing this family, or should I say *not* knowing this family, I had no idea what to expect. Except maybe chaos.

Everyone began filing into the church and damn, you would have thought a politician or local celebrity had died. There was a long line of people waiting to get inside the building, and over half were the family. I walked past most of the other sisters that had already viewed Granny in the casket and had taken their seats. When it was our turn to head to the front, I went up with Momma, Charles, and Dimples. Momma was tense and trying to hold back her tears. When we finally made it up to the casket, we all peered in and there she was, looking like she was asleep. Before I could figure out what was different, Charles's ignorant ass said, "Dat don't look like Granny ta me. She ain't never wore no makeup." He sounded just like a moose trying to whisper.

Dimples looked at me and just gave me the eye, we never had to say anything.

"I mean, hell, she looks like they put pancake batter on her face." He went on until Momma elbowed him hard in what I think, and hope, were his balls. We headed over to our seats while the rest of the place settled in and the service began.

When the minister got up to speak, he asked me to come up and sing a song for "The Grand Occasion." Even now I ask myself why I wasn't automatically put on the program. Although it caught me off guard, I stood up and walked what seemed an eternity up to the front of the church and to the mic.

I looked over at the musician and saw it was my friend Tony, the one who had always accompanied me, so I knew I was in good hands. I looked up at all the faces I hadn't seen in years and many more I hadn't ever seen before, and although my nerves were rattling, all I could think of was that sweet lady who had always given me peace while painting the house, given me courage while telling me jokes, and loved me in her own wonderful way. This would be my farewell to her.

I started the song "There's Not a Friend Like the Lowly Jesus," and the entire crowd looked up at once.

"None else could heal all our soul's diseases, no not one, no not one..."

With my song, I could actually feel the healings and mendings of relationships ease through the room. I could see cousins, brothers, sisters, and grandkids thinking about issues.

"Jesus knows all about our struggles, He will guide till the day is done..."

For the first time, even through the tears and sorrow for the loss of the matriarch lying in this place, I felt a warmth in the room with people who had never liked each other and fought over everything. As I started the vamp and final part of the song, I saw Charles holding his head down, trying to hide the tears as he held onto Momma. Aunt

Rachel jumped up and waved her huge church fan, and Aunt-Sister yelled out, "Yes, Lord, sang it, Terrell!" She put her arms around Aunt Ruby and Uncle Roosevelt, who were so taken by the moment they sat there simply comforting each other.

After I closed the song and started walking to my seat, I walked down that aisle as if it were a totally different path than I had taken walking up there. I could see smiles, tears, joy, and pain in the faces of family and friends. But most of all, there was a look of satisfaction and respect for me. It was then and there that I realized I had something for the world, something to change the world with. For if I could change the cold hearts of these insane people, then I would be able to change the world. And not just my voice, but what was inside of me, would translate through song, and that notion was phenomenal. It needed to be heard around the world.

When I sat down next to Dimples, she took my hand with tears in her eyes. I looked up and the minister kept looking at me, saying "My, my, my...."

All at once, the church erupted in a spirit-filled praise, all across the building. He looked at me and smiled, shaking his head from side to side.

I could feel the presence of something bigger than any of us there filling the room, and as everyone else started to leave the church, I felt a tap on my shoulder.

"Hello, darling." When I turned around, I looked into the familiar friendly face of Sweetie Pie.

"I am so proud of the young man you've become, and I want you to keep going all the way." With tears in her eyes, she took my hand and pressed something tightly into it, then kissed me on my cheek and walked away. When she was gone, I looked into my hand to see what she had placed into it. There were five crisp hundred-dollar bills and a note that said: "California is waiting for you, darling."

All I could do was sob. I saw more than money: it was not only kindness, it was the beginning of an opportunity for me to see the world.

Yes, this was truly the beginning.

chapter 52

What Did You Get for Christmas?

I loved being around Betty and Anie during the Thanksgiving and Christmas season, especially since Granny was gone and there was no one there to cook our family dinners. Anie had just dropped me and Betty off at her house where we were gonna get into our monthly ritual: pizza, wings, and horror movies. Just as we got all settled in and changed into our comfortable clothes, we heard a knock on the door.

"Terrell, can you go get that, please?" Betty asked.

"Hey, there," said the man at the door. I really didn't know what to say. It was like looking in a mirror, but thirty years into my future.

"Is Betty here?" he asked. He walked right past me, bringing two little girls in with him. I just stood there with the door open.

"June Bug, what's up?" Betty looked over at me with sadness in her eyes. "Close the door, Terrell," she said in the most caring voice. I did and went and sat back down next to her.

"What's going on, Betty? It's snowing like hell out there."

"It sure is, Daddy," one of the little girls said.

I almost shit on the couch. This was Kevin, my "father," and he was here with these two little girls calling him Daddy. I'd heard he'd gotten married to a woman who had five children, but seeing this for myself was so different. How could this man live with himself, knowing that his only son was right here in front of him, just walking by me and into the kitchen like I was the invisible man, then leaving those two girls in the room with me.

Luckily, even though I was in shock, I have always been blessed with level thinking, so I stayed calm and assessed the situation, like I do today. Ask any of my friends and they will tell you I can party with the best of them, but when I need to be calm and level-headed, I can be. Here was such a situation. I listened calmly as Kevin's stepdaughters, two of the most beautiful little girls I had ever seen, by the way, with long hair down their backs and very fair skin, talking about all the gifts their "father" had bought them.

Kevin came back out of the kitchen. "Let's go, girls," he said. "I'll catch you later, Betts, just wanted to come and say hi. I gotta pick my wife up from the hospital."

I still couldn't believe this man was ignoring me like I wasn't even there, talking like he wanted to hurt me with every syllable.

Kevin and his wife had just had a baby girl, he said, and when I heard that, I felt numb. I didn't know what to do, so I just sat there for what felt like hours. How could someone be so cold? It was surreal, like one of those out-of-body experiences people say they have on the operating table. This was the man who raped my mother when she was a little girl not much older than these girls here, and he was in charge of two gorgeous little ones and a baby girl who just came into the world. It made me sick.

Kevin went on and on and on and on until one of the girls asked me, "What did *you* get for Christmas?"

I was shocked back into the room. I didn't even know how to answer that. I looked up at her and could see it wasn't a question, it was a competition. I was speechless because this beautiful girl who had no idea how tough this situation already was for me was just doing what kids do. But in this case, every word she said felt like it was being delivered on purpose by a full-grown adult.

"Terrell got a trip out to California where he is going to become a big star," Betty said in all earnestness to the two girls, who looked at her like she was speaking a foreign language.

I looked at her and smiled. Betty wasn't usually one to save the day, but today she knew exactly the right thing to say.

chapter 53

California

Anie and Betty dropped me off at the church at three in the morning, and when we got out of the car, Betty was already having her say.

"I'm not sure how having *my* Momma get out of bed to take *you* to this church at three o'clock in the morning is okay, but *oh, well*. When *I* was a kid and needed to go somewhere, she'd make me catch the bus...or *walk!*"

I still don't know why she came along for the ride when all she did was complain about having to get up, but she probably wanted to make sure I knew I was getting special treatment.

By this time, Betty was becoming more and more strange. It seemed like she was living inside different people, and looking back now, she was most definitely bipolar, which come to think of it, probably everyone in my family was. But I couldn't and wouldn't think about any of that right now. I was going on my first trip across the country and to me, it might as well have been to the moon. I kissed them both and started to run inside when the horn blared.

Beep-beep!

"Yo bag, Terrell!" Anie got out of the car and ran up to the door of the church with my bag, huffing and puffing. I kissed her again and waved at Betty, but she wasn't even looking, so I ran into the church.

Inside, everyone was sleepy but excited, most of them also traveling to the moon for the first time.

"I hope everyone has all their belongings together and hasn't forgotten anything because it's too late now. California, here we come!" Jerome headed towards the exit and onto the bus waiting outside.

"Okay, you lovely people, let's get on the bus, we have a plane to catch," Linda Craft, our tour manager, said. She was Jerome's cousin and didn't play around when it came to organization.

Finally, everyone was on the bus and we were off. Marsha sat next to me. "Boy, can you believe it?" she asked with a yawn.

"I can," I answered, thinking about Granny and the feeling I had at the funeral. "I actually can."

Marsha's head quickly hit my shoulder and she was asleep in no time. For the rest of the ride I gazed out the window.

* * *

"Ladies and gentlemen, please fasten your seatbelts for takeoff," the captain said while the stewardesses closed and locked the doors.

This was the first time I had flown in years, but surprisingly enough, I wasn't afraid at all. I was more anxious than anything. Marsha, on the other hand, was like a flea caught in a spiderweb.

"Jesus, Terrell, I think we about ta fall out the sky...Lord!" She clutched my arm with a grip that was like how a powerlifter might grip a set of dumbbells.

"Marsha, girl, calm down, it's gonna be okay," Jerome said, laughing with the lady who was seated next to him.

"Four hours of this," Debbie Adams said from the rear of the plane and that made us all laugh, which released a tiny bit of Marsha's tension.

We finally arrived in LA, and as soon as the last of our bags came off the belt, we headed off to the hotel.

"Listen up, everyone. I want to stress to all of you that we are most definitely not in Buffalo anymore. Even though it looks like paradise, it's also a place where they will kill you as quick as look at you, so stick together and don't start any fights because I can't help you if you do." Jerome was mainly looking at the band, who were known for horsing around with people in public for pranks.

I didn't hear a thing he said after that because I was gazing at palm tree after palm tree, thinking about how beautiful the scenery was compared to Buffalo. Everything looked so big, and as the driver took us through Beverly Hills, I was speechless, looking at some of the houses there. I couldn't believe people lived like this.

"This is nothing like that TV show," the bus driver said, and everyone laughed.

I went into a trance and was somewhere else. My senses were so filled, I didn't think I could take any more in, which was when the driver said, "Here we are now, turning on to Hollywood Boulevard, where you will see the world-famous Walk of Fame. On the sidewalk are the stars of all your favorite performers, from Redd Foxx To Audrey Hepburn. If you look over to your right, you will see the Hollywood sign."

I did as I was told and when I did, it seemed like time stood still. I got a lump in my throat and my eyes starting to sting with tears. Trying to hold them back, I felt a thousand emotions boiling up inside me. Here I was, the Problem Child, the "mistake boy" from a dysfunctional family who barely acknowledged me. Looking at that Hollywood sign, I knew I had found my home and knew right then this was where I was supposed to be. Someday soon I was going to be here, all by myself, with not one single one of those people I grew up knowing, whether they loved me or not. I remember staring at that sign, not jabbering on about movies and movie stars like everyone else. I examined every letter until I said to myself, "I will see you again. That's a promise."

chapter 54

Bad Conditions

At the crack of dawn there was a knock on Candy and Tony's door. "Who is that at six o'clock in the morning?" Tony asked as Candy sat up on the bare mattress tucked into the corner of the cluttered apartment.

"Go get the door, Tony," Candy said.

Tony opened the door a crack to reveal Miss Laura, the apartment building manager. She gagged when she got a nose-full of the stench coming from inside that apartment but pressed on. "Is Candy here?"

"Yes, come on in, she's right over there."

Miss Laura hesitantly stepped into the darkened apartment and could faintly see Candy on the bed. She'd decided to take Candy and Tony under her wing when she found out that Candy had a condition, not really knowing how to place Tony, she just thought she would do a good deed and help these challenged young people out as best she could. Now she regretted her decision.

"I need to talk to you both," Miss Laura began, realizing this would be harder than she thought. She started off kind. "As you know, this is a four-plex and—"

"Uh, this is a what, Miss Laura?" Tony cut in.

Unlike Candy, Tony wasn't "officially" special needs but, as Charles once described him, "His elevator doesn't go all the way up." Or "The house is full but no one's allowed to go upstairs."

"It means there are four apartments here, yours and three others," Miss Laura said with the tone of a schoolteacher. "We all need to make an effort to live peacefully with each other, and if you'll remember, I made a point of saying that when you all signed the lease. But I'm afraid the other tenants have expressed some concerns." She paused here, not really knowing how to formulate what she was about to say without hurting their feelings. Tony and Candy stared at her with wide-eyed innocence. It was no use. She had to tell them. "Everyone's complaining about the odor of feces coming from your apartment." She gagged again then took a hanky out from her purse, covering her nose and mouth with it.

Confused, Tony asked in a humble, sweet voice, "I'm sorry, what do you mean?"

Miss Laura blinked, thinking she'd been pretty darn clear, then tried again. "There's an aroma of human waste permeating throughout the dwelling." As soon as she said it, she realized her mistake.

"What?" Candy asked naively from the stained mattress.

It was no use. "The place smells like shit and piss."

"Oh! I'm sorry, I forgot to flush the toilet this morning," Tony responded quickly in an attempt to cover the best way he knew how.

"I hardly doubt it was from missing one flush, Tony. And anyway, can y'all please turn on some lights so I can see Candy when I talk to her?" Miss Laura asked while putting on her glasses, like that was gonna help.

"Oh, yeah, you know, we haven't had a chance to get the electricity turned on yet," Tony said.

"What you mean? You've been in this damn apartment for two months," Miss Laura said with some anger in her voice, although she was trying her best to be nice. She was also trying to make sure her handbag didn't hit the floor, knowing it would never be the same if it so much as grazed the dark green, almost-black wood floors that were once off-white. "I wouldn't recognize this place if I hadn't rented it to you myself," she said in disgust and, knowing she wasn't going to get anywhere, dropped the bomb she came to drop. "I'm gonna need you to find some other place to live so I can salvage the relationship with my other tenants and what's left of this apartment."

"Do what to the relationship?" Tony asked, scratching his head and trying to keep the dingy sheet he was wrapped in from falling off and exposing his scrawny frame.

"Oh my God. Get y'all shit and get out. You got one week." Miss Laura stormed out of the apartment and made a beeline for the front door, hoping she wasn't going to throw up on the doorstep.

There was a silence after she left that neither of them knew how to fill, both trying to sort out the information they were just given as well as their own feelings about it.

"Where we gonna go, Tony?" Candy asked helplessly as she sat on that dirty bed in that terrible apartment. It might be wretched, but to them it was home.

chapter 55

Everything Hollywood

"Hey, so I've been wondering why people always call you Terrell and not Damon," Charmaine said to me as we settled into our seats before first period. "Hello? Earth to yo deaf ass."

"I'm sorry, Charmaine, I'm just in a daze after that trip." I laughed. "It's like I can finally see the plan for my life. I mean, it's not exactly mapped out, but I can see that it's where I'm supposed to go. I don't even know what the first steps will be, but I'm ready to take them when they show up."

"Well damn, you seem like you done had a revelation or something." She held her head back with a big smile, and I laughed. We could never be serious. "Dude, look at your book."

We both looked down at the brown paper bag cover we all had on our school textbooks and saw that I had written Hollywood all over it, in different sizes and handwriting. I hadn't even really noticed I'd done it, like it wasn't even me writing it. But the only thing I could think about was Los Angeles and that damn Hollywood sign, since for me it truly was a sign. A sign that I was in the right place at the right time, doing the right things, and perhaps all the dysfunction in my family and the unattached way I had been raised, being completely different from the rest of them...maybe...just *maybe*...none of it was a mistake after all, and my life had a bigger, deeper purpose. Maybe.

chapter 56

Another Funeral

There was a lady down the street from us we used to call Miss Nell. She was known for having a bunch of drunks and street-type folk always coming in and out of her house. One day we heard she had lost her daughter to what they said was natural causes, but the poor girl weighed only about sixty pounds and was thirty-seven years old, so I'm not sure how the hell they got natural from that, but okay. Then again, I didn't really think too much about it because only God knew what kind of shit people would be saying about me. Anyway, Miss Nell asked if I would sing at her daughter's funeral, and since I was hot to sing anywhere I could, I agreed.

Luckily the funeral home was walking distance from Momma's house so if I didn't see Charles or his car out there I could to stop by and grab some clothes before getting the hell out. Edwin's Funeral Home was one of the more famous ones in Buffalo, at least with all the black people, because they ran specials all the time and accepted payment plans. Rumor had it they were able to do this because they would dump the bodies in more than one grave and steal the caskets back.

I walked up to the front door to the sweet sounds of an organ playing "Precious Lord." Two older ladies dressed in black were heading inside to the left. I followed them in, preparing myself mentally for all the sadness. There were about seven people in the place and the atmosphere was so peaceful, the kind where you might see doves being released and a preacher with a smile delivering a heartfelt eulogy that would end with "Job well done, thy good and faithful servant." That's when I glanced up at the casket and saw the well-dressed man lying inside it.

The usher had been watching and approached after seeing the confused look on my face. "Son, you look lost."

"I guess I kind of am. I'm supposed to be singing at my neighbor's daughter's funeral today. I think their last name is Duncan."

"Oh yes, I put all of those people on the other side of the funeral home where they would have their own entrance. I'll take you through."

"Bitch, why you have to leave us!" someone screamed as we got close to the doorway to the last room at the back.

"Momma, I can't do dis shit without you!" one of the young girls said from the back, yelling at the casket.

"Sit yo bad ass down. You was the reason she didn't make it, giving her stress all the time, all that damn stress."

"Geraldine, dammit, sit the hell down, talkin' to that girl like that at her momma's funeral."

What the hell had I walked into? Unlike the other place, this room smelled like the few drops of Olde English beer left at the bottom of the bottle in the summer heat for three days. It was packed with people, and not a fat person in the room. I'm sure the running diet was crack, judging by the fact that the fifty skeletons in the room had a grand total of seven teeth between them.

There was a young guy at the organ playing Rick James and Jodeci songs, and even though I wasn't sure if he and I would gel, I also knew it didn't matter to these folks one bit if we did or not.

"Hey, I'm Terrell. I'm supposed to sing at this funeral."

"What up, man. I'm Steve Jordan. Call me Stevie J. What you singin', church boy?" He went into the vamp of "Forever My Lady."

"I'm gonna sing "I'll Fly Away." You know that tune?"

"Nope, but we'll figure it out," he said, and I started the song. He clearly had no idea how to play it, but for some reason I knew he knew the song. The whole thing was pretty much a train wreck, but we made it sound like we planned it to sound like "Thriller."

It was like we weren't even there. That group of mourners was a million miles away. We got through it, and when we finished, Stevie J. looked at me, his eyes wide.

"Man, you can sing your ass off," he said, the held out his hand for me to shake. "I'm a producer, and I'm thinking you and me oughtta do some work together."

I was such a baby, I swear I had no idea what the hell being a producer meant, but I knew it had something to do with music, like what Jerome was doing with the Lighthouse Choir, so I was down.

"Sure, man, I'm trying to sing as much as I can these days. Let's do it."

"Sounds good. Now let's get our twenty bucks and get the fuck outta here."

Stevie was the perfect mix between street, church, bad boy, and gentleman. He knew exactly how to act and how to talk to people. A charmer, but full of street smarts. Perfect brotherhood for my churchy, square ass. Stevie J. and I started hanging out, doing music and shows together, and he introduced me to other singers and musicians. I knew this dude was going somewhere, and in some of the same ways I could also see that light over his head.

chapter 57

Where to Next?

By this time, Candy had gained so much weight she couldn't walk, so Tony had to be waiting on her hand and foot. After being kicked out, they had to think fast, which wasn't easy, so they did the only thing they could think of. Tony was pushing Candy in her wheelchair on their way to Willie's house, hoping they could stay there for a night or two until they figured it all out.

"Tony, I'm not sure this is the right way," Candy said, looking confused and not the least bit cold. Candy had little more than a thin blanket over her lap and Tony wasn't dressed to be walking outside in that cold Buffalo weather.

"I think it's just down here, Candy," Tony said, his teeth chattering.

An hour later they were still walking in circles, trying to figure out which way to go. Luckily, a kind lady coming back from the store saw them again and decided this couple must be in trouble.

She pulled over, rolled down her window, and leaned out. "Hey there, do you two need some help?" She saw the poor woman in the wheelchair trying to cover herself with a blanket that looked like it was almost frozen solid because Candy had already wet herself several times since they left.

"Well, we been trying to find Willie's house, but all I know is it's on Maston," Tony said. "Put the chair in the back of my truck and I'll help you find the place you're looking for."

Tony helped put the chair in the back of the car and the lady kept her promise, helping the two of them find the old house on the left side of the street. Ironically, there were no other houses left in four lots on either side.

The lady looked at the house and said, "Well, this has to be it. There are no other houses on this block," she said in disbelief that they were lost on a street with no other houses anywhere near the one they were looking for.

"Yes! That's were Daddy lives!" Candy said excitedly, finally having made it.

"You guys take care, okay?" The nice lady headed back to her truck, shaking her head and hoping they'd be all right. As she pulled away from the curb, she couldn't help but wonder why no one was helping them, two people who so obviously needed help.

chapter 58

The Live Recording

Jerome announced that the Lighthouse Choir would be recording live, so I was beyond excited when we started rehearsals for it. My excitement was short-lived when Jerome started passing out the names of the lead singers.

I'd been performing with them for months now, proving myself and doing well, I thought, so I was disappointed when he hadn't given me a main part for the recording. I was already leading a song with the choir, so what the hell?

"Okay, we're down to the last two, then we'll be done picking the songs for the recording." Paula Smith came up and presented her song to the choir. "I think A.G. should lead this one," she said.

A.G. was known as the man who not only had range but could and would kill a song every time. However, he already had one. I didn't say anything, but everyone could see the look on my face, especially Jerome, because he moved his attention in my direction. He saw me breathing hard and hesitated.

"Terrell, there is one more song and I am willing to give it to you, but I need to know you are going to be consistent. You realize that this is going to be a live recording, and it's not easy fixing mistakes in the studio."

I had had some issues with key changes and stuff in the past, but that was because of nerves since I was unable to hear where the musicians were going. I wasn't skilled enough yet to cover up mistakes on the spot like I can now.

"Jerome, I understand totally, and I'll work hard on whatever song you choose to give me. I'll make sure it's right."

He gave it some thought. I looked around the room and I could tell I was being supported by more than half the choir. He could sense it too. "Okay, Terrell, there's a song I have in mind and I am going to let you lead it. But I want it to be a duet with Kelly."

My face fell and everyone saw it. Kelly was a good singer; I just didn't want to sing with someone else. Still, I had to do what our leader asked, which was all part of being a professional, so I humbly said, "Gotcha, Jerome."

He gave me a look, knowing I was learning an important lesson that would follow me the rest of my life. Everyone else looked at me and then we all laughed. I really loved these people.

The day arrived, and the choir was ready. We had worked so hard on these songs and the church was packed. It seemed like everyone from Buffalo had come out to see the event. The crowd was in an uproar when we went marching across the stage. The entire church felt like it was on fire. And for me, it was like being in a dream. The thought hadn't really crossed my mind since I had been fixated on getting the song with Kelly right, but I guess this was the first time I would be recording professionally.

"Sometimes all you have to do is say 'I love you, Lord, I really do,'" Jerome said as he introduced me and Kelly. The song started and we let them have it. I was ready and so was she. It proved to be absolutely perfect, because you could hear that the two of us were working together, unlike sometimes when you hear two singers trying to out-sing each other and it turns out to be a screaming match.

We sang, and when the song ended, the crowd got to its feet. It was done and out there forever. My voice had been recorded and would be out there for everyone to hear, for years to come.

chapter 55

Vegas

"Hello, Candy, girl? How you doin? You sure you okay?" Momma was saying into the phone when I entered the house.

I had come by to let Momma know how the recording went and to get some more stuff I needed from my room. I was getting sick and tired of having half my shit there and the other half at Anie's, but I knew it was all going to be coming to an end very soon.

What I didn't know was that Candy and her friend Francine had decided to go to Vegas to try their hand at prostitution, which was what Dimples told me before I went into my old room. I laughed, thinking she was lying. I gathered my stuff quickly before anything hit the fan and headed out towards the front door just in time to hear Momma's reaction to the whole thing.

So I sat down and I'm waiting for the colors to fly that I know Momma is getting ready to put on the wall. The shit was about to hit the fan, of that I was sure, so I braced myself. Momma smiled over at me and gave me a nod and went back to her conversation.

"How are you doing out there? I hope you making some good money.... Oh, is that Francine I hear in the background?" Momma asked.

"*Yes, Momma, that's her,*" Candy said on the other end.

"Well, you tell her I said hello and to keep trying to get what you can out there. Oh, and make sure you listen to what she says, okay, honey?" Then Momma hung up the phone and said to me as she walked out the kitchen, "Y'all help yourself to what's in the fridge. I gotta go see how Charles is doing."

I sat there in a daze for a few minutes, blown away, until I eventually got up and walked out the door without saying anything to anyone. This was what Candy was now being subjected to? I had my own problems, but I couldn't help feeling like I was failing her too. Hell...did *anyone* care about *anyone* in this Godforsaken family?

A few weeks later Dimples told me Momma was all pissed off because all Candy brought home was seventy-five dollars.

chapter 60

Shot

It was early in the morning and I was waiting on the bus for school. I'm not sure what these thugs were doing up, or if they'd even been to sleep, but they were behind me doing what they do while I stayed as far away from them and as close to the bus sign as I could.

"Nigga, that bitch ain't shit," one of them, strutting around with his chest stuck out.

I remember thinking how much I hated that shit, acting like that. It just was so far removed from what I wanted in life. As I listened unintentionally to their conversation, I couldn't see the bus anywhere in sight, so I decided it wasn't a good idea to let them hang behind me, and maybe I should walk a block to the next stop. I moved just a bit to the right and I heard some tires screeching.

"Move, nigga!" a guy screamed from the car as I tried to get out of the way. But it was too late. He was spraying the corner with bullets. It happened so fast I didn't have time to think.

I heard them scream and as I started looking for a way out, that was when I noticed the back of my leg was on fire. I saw a lady walking fast towards her house and said, "Ma'am, can you please help me? I think I've been shot. I'm not like the guys you see on the corner, I promise." She took one look at me and decided I was right. This being pre-cellphone days, she let me come in and use the phone.

"Momma, it's Terrell. I think I been shot," I said as I bled all over the nice lady's kitchen floor.

This was the first time, without a shadow of a doubt, I had ever felt Momma really cared about me. The good thing was, I was only a block from Buffalo General Hospital.

"*What? Where are you?*" she screamed into the phone.

"I'm at a lady's house near the hospital Betty works at and—"

"*Well get yo ass down there right now!*"

I thanked the lady and hobbled over to the hospital. I could still walk, although the part of my leg where I felt the wound was pretty numb. Probably a good thing. When I got there, Betty greeted me at the emergency room. As luck would have it, she was working that day and Momma had gotten to her just in time. Right before the entrance door closed, I heard the exhaust pipe from Anie's car pulling up, so I knew she was coming close behind.

"Momma is on her way, and everybody else is too," Betty said. "Come on, have a seat down here and we'll take you back." She sat me down in a wheelchair to take me to the examination room.

Anie came running in as if I had been shot three times in the chest and was a bleeding mess on the floor. "How's my babe? Lord Jesus, what happened!? You okay?"

I started to explain the situation when the security guard came inside and said to Anie, "Ma'am, you left your car right at the entrance. Could you please come back outside and move it before it gets towed?"

"Man, if you tow my damn car I'll beat yo ass. I'm lookin after my baby. Ain't this the emergency room? Well this is an emergency. You better get out my face before they gon' be needin' a bed for you."

Betty and Anie took me back so a doctor could have a look while I explained what had happened. A few minutes later a nurse came in and made sure I wasn't bleeding and got my vitals while Anie held my hand.

"I'll go and get the papers we need you to sign before the doctor comes in. I'll be right back."

"Damn gang members. My babe, you coulda been killed! Damn glad it was just your leg," Anie went on.

"Mister Carter, I need you to give me a few pieces of information. Mother's name?" she asked, and I gave it to her. "Father?"

It was the first time anyone had really asked me. Luckily, I was always a quick thinker and was prepared to give some remark that would soften the situation. "Well, ma'am, my father is—"

A voice that sounded like a mature reflection of my own filled the room. "I'm him. Kevin Burder is my name."

The nurse wrote that down and was about to fill in some more spaces on her form, but when she looked up and saw the look on all our faces, she put her pen down and left the room.

I almost jumped off the stretcher. It was Kevin standing there. All I remember was that the sound in the room went mute and I felt as if I were looking through a telescope, only at him. I didn't know how to respond. Do I smile? Cry, like I'm doing now as I write this? Or just ignore him like he did to me all the years up until now? Well, I didn't have time to do any of those things because Anie started crying before anyone could, loud and almost down on her knees.

"Lord, Jabo, I know you heard that in heaven and you smiling this day!"

I just sat there in shock. Happy, joyous, and in pain all at the same time while Anie praised the heavens and Jabo most annoyingly.

I knew Kevin had his reasons for not admitting the truth. I mean, would you? But I never thought the day would come when he would say it out loud, to me or anyone else. I hadn't even prepared myself or imagined it to be a possibility because it felt so farfetched. In fact, I didn't even feel the wound anymore.

All of a sudden I forgot why I was at the hospital, and everything I ever knew paled in comparison. Kevin had just said, "I'm his father."

chapter 61

A New Home

When someone gets shot in the movies, it looks like a really big deal, but my wound was healing fast. They had sent me over to Betty's because Anie was in the hospital having some minor surgery done on her foot and didn't want me to be alone at the house. She said it was because of the bullet wound, but I think it had more to do with the fact that she didn't trust a teenager around her knick-knacks. I certainly hadn't had a very good history with them, that's for sure.

"The rug in the bathroom always needs to face the window because it catches too much light when it's the other way," Betty said after popping in a movie. "Otherwise it will fade from the sunlight."

What does that have to do with anything? I thought, though before she could react to the look on my face, someone knocked on the door.

"Open up in there!" a mysterious, but familiar voice said.

"Coming." Betty jumped up and opened the door. "Hey there, man."

It was Kevin.

This was turning into a common thing, him popping up everywhere I was.

"Hey, June." Betty escorted him over to the loveseat, which was right near my head.

"What up, man?" he said playfully.

It took a second for me to speak.

"Hey." The dry, crackly sound came out of my mouth. Then I realized that I was more afraid of what I should be calling him than I was afraid of him, period.

"How you feeling, old man?" he asked me and the tension could be cut with a sword.

"I'm doing great," I said with the most masked, fake smile I have ever mustered.

"Well, that's good news, because I talked to my wife and we both decided you should come and live with us. I know that it's been difficult for you, bouncing around and not knowing where you belong, so we want to end all of that."

Betty looked at me with just as much surprise on her face as I'm sure I had.

"When were you thinking of me coming?" I asked.

"That's why I'm here."

For the first time in my life I was speechless. Any one of my closest friends who may be reading this now is probably more shocked at that than anything they might have read in this story so far.

Betty and I got my things together and off we went. There were obvious thoughts and concerns on Betty's face, but her state was already one foot on crazy and the other on a banana peel.

"Love you, Terrell, see you later," was all she said as we got into the car.

I remember thinking that the tone of her voice spoke so much louder than the words.

* * *

When we got to Kevin's house the sweetest, most caring woman gave me a warm hug. "I'm Jewel, your step-mother," she said, and with a big smile, she introduced me to the children. I was surprised I actually liked them all.

She and I eventually developed a good relationship, I liked her, I trusted her, and I was happy there.

A week or two after moving in with them, Kevin called me down to the basement where he had a studio. I was even more blown away to learn that this man was musically inclined as well. When he picked up the guitar and started playing, my jaw dropped. Then he started to sing, and it was all new to me. He had a good voice, not like mine though. Unlike me, he could play as well as I could sing.

He started singing words that just came off the top of his head, words he had wanted to say to me but was unable to come right and out and say.

"I understand that it's been so many years and I've wanted to reach out to you but didn't know how. I hope you see it in your heart to let me in because I love you."

I had the mic in my hand and I was pretty sure he was expecting me to respond and so, I thought it would be best if I just said all the things I *should* say and not some of the things I *wanted* to say.

"It has been hard but I'm happy you and I can finally meet and put it all behind us."

Then I realized how difficult this would be after I saw who was coming into the house. None other than Bonnie.

I had seen Bonnie in the past from going to church with Anie and Betty, and on occasion Bonnie would come as well. When she was around, she would treat me well, mostly by cracking jokes, but this was the first time we all were going to be in one room. Kevin took over the jam and started singing and playing. It got to a point where it was more for the room than me.

"I'm glad y'all are doing good," Bonnie said, and the mood started to change. "It's got to be a lot better than being over there with Mae and *her* dumb ass."

"I hate that bitch," Kevin chimed in and put the guitar down.

"The only thing that woman was to my father was an expense," Bonnie said right to my face. This was the first time I'd ever been alone with the two of them, and I am glad it hadn't been earlier.

"Then your momma and her pissy ass got the nerve to make sure she got a check after he died," Kevin said, as if Jabo would be able to use it after he was buried in the ground.

This went on for a long while, them going on and on about Momma, Candy, and Charles so badly, then Bonnie slipped up and explained what had really happened to the houses on Guilford.

"I would have been able to keep the house over there if Mae had agreed to stay in there and pay rent like I asked her to. She just up and left the house and didn't even tell anyone that she was leaving. Left all these bills on me and the taxes got behind and I lost all three of the houses. I'll never forgive her for it."

The story I'd heard so many times from just about everyone was the one I told in an earlier chapter, that Bonnie made us all leave. She had lost everything by being greedy.

After about an hour and a half of the Mae-bashing, I excused myself, catching this last sentence before I grabbed a few of my things out of the room I was sharing with one of the kids and tiptoed out the side door: "Remember the time we were all going to get groceries and that bitch Mae..."

As I got to the end of the driveway, Raquel, one of the little girls who I adored and was the one who had taunted me about my Christmas gift, looked up at me with innocent eyes. "Where are you going, brother? Can I come?"

I had grown close with his family and actually hated leaving them. "I'm going to a rehearsal," I told her, knowing I'd never, as long as I lived, want to be in Kevin's presence again. Even though Mae wasn't the best and, sure, Candy *was* pissy, and they might have done all the horrible things they said about them, they were still the ones who kept me when his sorry, raping, pedophile, no-good ass walked out and couldn't be a man and admit... Oh, wait, I've forgiven him.

But I as sure as hell will never forget. Let's stop there.

chapter 62

You Gotta Go

Anie was out of the hospital but decided to hang out over at Betty's, which I didn't want to do seeing that Betty was turning into the crypt keeper, so I decided I'd sneak back over to Anie's and stay there by myself. I had just had a good meal and was lying on the bed watching some TV when the phone rang. I snatched it up before I thought about it because I was half asleep.

"Hello," I said, my voice groggy.

"Who is this? I must have the wrong number."

I don't know why, but I'm not sure why I didn't even think about the fact that Kevin would probably let them know I had left.

The next thing I knew there was a walker coming through the front door. "What the hell you think you doing over here, Terrell? You know I told you I didn't want anyone coming in and out of here when I wasn't here because you may let Snowdrop out." Snowdrop was Anie's sometimey cat that didn't really respond to anyone, even her, until it was time for her to eat. That cat would hide from me, so I knew it was Anie just not wanting me to be over there.

"I didn't want to hang out over there with you because Betty acts crazy towards me sometimes," I tried to explain.

"Well, you ain't never got to come over there no more and I'll be okay," Betty said.

Jesus, I see where I get all of the crazy, quick comebacks I like to claw back with. The fact was, Anie didn't want me to be in her place alone, and this was all beginning to be too much anyway.

"You got somewhere to go?" Anie asked as I walked out the door. She loved me with all of her heart and didn't want to see me be anything but a success, but I understood that her only source of anything really was Betty and that would be poison even to God's ears.

One day I'll tell you the Anie and Betty story from their point of view. This shit was dysfunctional full circle.

I looked back at her and said, "Yes, I have somewhere to go." I closed the door and got into the cab that was taking me right back to Mae and Charles's. I did not want to go.

chapter 63

The Blowup

I had finally graduated, and even though no one came to the ceremony, I felt like it had been the thing that had really been holding me back. I had been back at Momma's house about three weeks. I was sitting out on the porch thinking about Hollywood, Granny, and all of the music I wanted to do with Stevie J., when a van pulled up. It was a medical van, some kind of home health aide or something. They lowered the step down and out popped Candy, being pushed by an attendant.

"Hi, Terrell," she said, and I was more happy to see her in that moment than I ever had been before. I thought how crazy life had been for me in the last few years, but I knew it had to be even worse for her.

"I'm going to sit out here with you if that's okay," Candy said.

"You know it is!"

Her attendant wheeled her next to the chair I was sitting in.

"Thank you, Charles," she said to the guy, who smiled at her in a way that seemed flirty.

His name would be Charles. Shit, I couldn't get away from that bastard.

"Son, I'm so proud of you. I know you are out there singing and stuff," Candy said.

"Yeah, it's been rough, but I really do feel like there is something else out there for me."

"There is more for you than what's here," she said. "The rest of us, we gonna be doing this shit forever and that's it."

I was floored. Candy wasn't the type to use large words or take you over the river and through the woods, she just said what was in her heart, and although it was simple, it was so true. We both knew I would die if I stayed here with these people, and all I would ever look forward to would be the end. We laughed almost until the sun went down and as simple as it was, this was the most meaningful time I had ever spent with the woman who started it all. Or had it all started for her, I should say. Sweet, innocent Candy. And although it didn't feel like she was or could be, she was my mother, and was guiding and teaching me in this moment everything I needed to know and hear.

We went inside the house still high and in good spirits only to have it all come crashing down. Charles came in drunk, slamming the door behind us. "I guess you just gonna heat the whole outside with my money," he said as he staggered into the room.

"I can't stand him," Candy said to me and I guess it was loud enough that his drunk ass heard it in the other room.

"I can't stand your stankin' ass either, and I wish your rotten ass would just die."

Dimples came running out of her room just in time to see what was happening.

"Come on, Daddy," Dimples said, trying to defuse the situation.

"Don't Daddy me. I hate both of they stupid asses. Why don't you just get the hell out of my house, you pissy-ass bitch. And take ya faggot-ass, no-sangin' son with you. Runnin' around here screamin' and hollerin' calling that shit sangin.' Everybody know he a faggot and don't nobody do that shit but faggots."

My blood started to boil, and Dimples looked at me as if to say, "Please don't say anything." I couldn't help it. The time had come when I needed to let this monster know that his shit stank just like all of ours.

"You calling me a faggot but you got eight kids and only three of them will amount to anything. So what does that make you?" I shot back.

"It makes me better than yo punk ass."

"Well, it would to you when you're an ignorant old dumb-ass man with no self-respect and none for even your own family, stealing your uncle's wife while he lay on his sick bed!" I shouted, and I may as well have called his mother a bitch. He jumped out of bed and went to the closet, while Dimples ran in to stop him. "I'mma blow your goddamn brains out, talking to me like that, bitch-ass boy."

Charles had never threatened to shoot me before. I turned around to see him trying to get to the closet. I'm not sure how Candy got out of the kitchen and down the back steps so quick, but she headed to the neighbor's house and I soon followed. I sure as hell wasn't going to stick around and find out if he really would shoot me.

"I'm gonna kill that faggot-ass boy!"

"Kiss my ass, you miserable old bastard!" I yelled as I ran through the neighbor's yard, not looking back at all.

chapter 64

The Escort

I was playing an album, Ron Winans's *Family & Friends 3*, and I took a look at the inside of the cover. I saw a manager's number and decided to call and talk to him to see if he could point me in the right direction—or in any direction. I didn't care what I had to do. Not only had the time come, but I really wanted and needed to get out of Buffalo.

The manager, Erik Williams, told me he was starting up a management company and asked me to sing over the phone. He was immediately blown away and told me if I could get to Detroit, he would love to work with me. Now the question was...how did I get there?

The next morning, I got up early and went to a dealership to get me a car—with no job. The Ford dealership didn't really care about none of that because I didn't care, and I knew I'd figure everything out later.

Thankfully everyone was out of the house when I went and gathered all my shit, or whatever I could get in the back and trunk of the car. Everything else I just left there because I didn't want anything that couldn't come with me. As I walked out the door and slammed it behind me, I knew I'd never return to that godforsaken place.

I was headed to Detroit, Michigan. It wasn't Hollywood, but it was at least in the right direction—west. I packed the last things in my car, pulled out of the driveway, popped in my Clark Sisters cassette and headed for the highway.

That Ford Escort left the city limits never to return. I was jumping off of a mountain not knowing if there was a net on the other side and I didn't care because I expected to fly. As the scattered snowflakes turned to almost white-out conditions, I was driving and thinking, with nothing but excitement in my heart. I had no idea what tomorrow was going to bring, but I knew that whatever came out of it, it would be better than where I was leaving.

I drove and drove, I sang and smiled, until I realized that I had driven seven hours, pretty much now out of gas and money. The snow was coming down so hard and I was in a part of the city that was obviously more of a wooded area, but I couldn't be that far from Detroit because I had been driving for so long. Pulling into a gas station, I decided to ask the guy for directions and let him know where I was going.

"Hello there, sir," I said, trying to be as kind as possible. He looked like one of those mountain men I had seen in so many of the scary movies with Betty where I never knew what to expect but was always on guard.

"Hey there, son," he said with a huge smile and not one tooth in his head.

It took me by surprise so much that I actually stumbled a bit as I was about to speak. "I was wondering, sir, if you could help me with directions. I'm driving from Buffalo trying to find the inner city of Detroit."

"Son, what?" He held his hat on top of all that wooly hair on top of his head. "You're four hours out of the way from where you want to be going." He scratched his head.

"Oh, I must have made a wrong turn. Or didn't take the right turn." *Shit.* I didn't even have enough money to get thirty minutes out of the station so I knew I wouldn't make it four hours.

He pulled out an old map from behind the counter and started drawing a red line that appeared like it wasn't going to ever stop. I got scared and my mind started going immediately. The good thing was, because of the way I grew up, I always had a way of figuring things out. Well, almost always. This was one of those times I was stumped.

"Can I use the phone, please?" I asked. I had to call and find some way of getting gas money sent here to this station. This was before QuickPay and iPhones and all that shit, and nobody I called answered because it was two o'clock in the morning.

"Young man, you seem to be in a bit of trouble," he said in the kindest way possible.

"Yessir, I am. I'm trying to figure out what I need to do. I have no money, and no one is answering their phone."

"Welp," he said in that country-road way then continued, "this is my station. I can fill your tank up and give you about fifty dollars. That should get you to where you are going. That is, if you don't make another wrong turn." Then he laughed so loud, like Boss Hogg from *The Dukes of Hazzard,* that it almost made me mad. But the reality was, I was so grateful for this man's generous gesture.

"Thank you so much, sir, I can't tell you how much I appreciate it."

"Just remember me when you get rich and famous," he said and laughed again. Now the funny thing was, looking back, I hadn't told this man anything about me, so how would he know about my dream? Well, another proof to me that God sends in angels just when you need one.

This new-life thing was off to a good start and I didn't realize it, but it was only going to get better, if I just walked in it. As I drove off, I waved back at the nice man and headed off in the right direction, this time Detroit bound.

chapter 65

Detroit and Beyond

True to its name, the Escort escorted me straight onto the stages of gospel legend Fred Hammond for four years, where I learned how to harmonize, vocalize, and perform in the studio. Then it was on to hook back up with Stevie J., who had become a star, going on to work with P. Diddy—still Puff Daddy at that time. I worked under Stevie J. for a year, and with him, went to LA to do some work under Quincy Jones, who eventually signed me as a writer. From that platform I worked with everybody from Beyoncé to Christina Aguilera, Deborah Cox, and Patti Labelle.

I wrote and sang with Whitney Houston, even on the last day she ever performed. I then went on to the most amazing Tyler Perry play days where I really got my start and the acting bug bit me—hard. Madea was hot underground and it made me an instant success and hometown hero.

My film debut was in *Diary of a Mad Black Woman*, Tyler Perry's first movie, where I sang the song "Father Can you Hear Me." More film roles, big and small, like *Think Like a Man Too*, were things that kept me afloat when I was looking for my next big thing auditioning and trying to make it in LA.

Since leaving Buffalo, I hadn't seen any of them for years. I thought of never looking back as my way of surviving, and it worked. Slowly but surely those awful memories died or simply faded into nothingness in my mind.

The deaths came back to back. First Kevin died of cancer, and on his deathbed he wanted to talk to me. He called Anie and asked her to call me. All she said was, "He wants to talk to you." Knowing her, I expected her to tell me calling him was right thing to do. Instead she just said, "Whatever you think is best, I'll stand behind you."

I thought about it. If he had truly wanted to say he was sorry or make any kind of amends that didn't include trying to make me a part of his patchwork family, he had had nineteen years to do it.

"I'm going to pass," was all I said. "Let him just go to wherever he's going." I could hear the disappointment in her voice, but she was satisfied that I'd made the right decision for me.

Not long after, they lost Candy to natural causes. I spoke to her the last day she could talk, and she said, "I love you, my son. I know more about you than you think. Even more than you know about yourself." I didn't know then it would be the last time I talked to her. And so the rest of them left this world, one after the other: Anie, Charles, Gerry, Sweetie-Pie, Tony, Mrs. Mary, all of the neighbors, and most of the friends. Dimples and I will always remain close. Tasha and I have a love-hate relationship that I hope gets better with time, but there is a disconnect that just seems to keep us apart. I've tried to have a relationship with Kevin's other daughters but when I see them, I think of him. Nothing personal but that's still just a bit much for me.

chapter 66

The Audition

I'd been in the business for years now and things were always up and down, which is just how the business is. One day you're up, the next you're down, as the famous song says. I had been auditioning for a while, yet things weren't working. Then I got the call to meet the great writer/director Lee Daniels. He was the creator of *Precious* and the hit series *Empire* and *Star*.

I was to audition for *Star*, the role of a rapist and stepfather to one of the girls. As I walked in knowing he would be there, I was nervous, but I was hoping that this was it. His sister Leah Daniels-Butler was the casting director, and I had seen her before, so she was bringing me back.

"Hello, everyone," I said as I walked into the room.

"Hey, Terrell," the siblings said together, as they often do. "You're not right for this part," Lee said. "You look too much like a model and not enough like a person who would be a rapist."

My first thought was, *You don't know who my father was.*

I just nodded and got ready to leave when he said, "Why don't you read for me anyway, because you never know."

I read the role he gave me, and he was impressed. "Your amazing acting skills, voice, and size actually make me believe you. I'm surprised I didn't know you already, or you would be working for me. I'll keep you in mind now, though, for sure."

It was as if a heavy weight had just fallen on top of me. I was *that* close and it was snatched right away in front of my eyes. In the elevator I said, "On to the next." In this town, nobody actually ever remembers when they say they will.

I needed to work, so I accepted a touring show, but was miserable out on the road with a director who was the worst person ever. He was full of drama, arrogant as hell, and lowballed me when it came to paying me my worth. Then I got a text from my agent:

"I have an audition for you. You need to put yourself on tape tonight."

Since I wasn't in LA to go in for the audition, I did what is known as a self-tape. The part was for Lee Daniels and *Empire*, playing the boyfriend of Jussie Smollett and nephew of the great Phylicia Rashad. I worked on that tape with my friend La'Myia Good, sister of Meagan Good, who happened to be on the show with me.

"Bro-bro, come on, you can do better than that. Get it together!"

"I know, let's try it one more time."

"That's the one," she said, and we hurried and sent it off.

"Thank you, sis."

There was no way I could sleep with this happening. I had a feeling I would get the call. I knew I was perfect for this.

The next evening, we were at the theater and my manager called and said the magic words: "You got it."

It was happening, and at that moment I knew I was on a different path. I had gone through heartache on so many levels, heartbreak dangers, seen and unseen, but it didn't matter. None of it mattered. I was here and this was my life.

chapter 67

Empire, Part Two

So there I was, in New York City at the Ritz-Carlton Hotel, waiting for my publicist to let me know the car had arrived to take me to the premiere of *Empire*. I had now worked with Phylicia Rashad, sung "Born to Love U" to Jussie Smollett, and been bumped up to series regular. What a wild ride indeed. And you'll remember it was also the night I found out Momma died. When I heard that, it suddenly became clear to me that no matter what life throws at you, no matter your circumstances, no matter how bad things look or how low the perception of yourself and your own life might be, life goes on and there is always hope. You can go to sleep one night with no way out and wake up the next morning with the answer sitting right in your face. Or the key to the first door of many that will eventually bring you to the answer.

Which is why I didn't let Momma ruin my night. After that fleeting thought, *Thank you, Momma, for ruining my night*, I actually looked out onto the New York skyline, with its shiny lights and promises of dreams that become reality, and thought instead, *Thank you,*

Momma, for making me fight. Thank all of you for making me fight harder than most to realize my dreams. I did it, I arrived, and I did it with barely any encouragement from anyone in my family.

I have to admit that the remnants of Guilford Avenue—Bonnie, Charles, Kevin, and all the rest of them—have never strayed far from my fight to have great relationships, the understanding of forgiveness, and trusting true love. I have learned to forgive them, and not just from my own point of view.

Writing about these people has opened up an entire dimension inside my heart of forgiveness I had no idea existed. I forgave people for exactly who and what they were, even when the situation seemed like it should be obvious as to why someone should apologize or why they should know and see the light. It's really hard to do, but try to forgive and understand how *they* look at it. I'm not saying it's right or that it's going to make it easier because, trust me, the rollercoaster of emotions, the bad relationships, self-discoveries, scandals, truths, rumors, tabloids, and loss of love I endured before *Empire* is an entirely different story. Maybe I'll just have to tell that to you one day as well.

In the meantime, you might agree with me now that nothing is by chance, that the Big Bang Theory of planets colliding and creating life that creates more life out of nothingness is a fable. That if I hadn't had all those difficulties in my life, I wouldn't have the depth of feeling and the heart for people that I have now. I wouldn't be the artist I am, the songwriter I am, the person I am. There is no way it was merely a coincidence that my voice was my ticket out of the swamp. It was meant to be. My voice, acting abilities, looks, and anything else are all just a platform to bring people to me for their healing. If I go on to become a huge star in the process that would be great, however that isn't the promise that I was put here for. I was brought here so that others can have a place to go and to be an example for those who need a role model. I'm here to compassionately heal and help usher people in the right direction. Dealing with all that I have was only to prepare me. I have pretty much seen it all in one form or another. I had to go through it.

When things don't quite go my way and doors that I had hoped would fling open close—that job, or that relationship, or a friendship that disappears right in front of my eyes, I can look up and say "God, I know you got me. You see I'm that little boy that no one wanted to claim properly, the one who came from the handicapped little girl who everyone laughed at and said the meanest things to. I'm the child they made fight to eat, sleep, and breathe, the child who saw all of the worst things, the child who was in the way."

Yep, that's me. And every day I awake, I am grateful to be that Problem Child.

acknowledgments

I would like to thank:

Mr. Tyler Perry
Darlene Meyers
Dr. George Smith
Stacey Thunes
Joyce Robinson
Karen Clark-Sheard
Peter Van Voorhis